THINK OUTSIDE THE ODDS

An Underdog's Toolkit for
Achieving the Impossible

THINK
OUTSIDE
THE ODDS

AN UNDERDOG'S TOOLKIT FOR
ACHIEVING THE IMPOSSIBLE

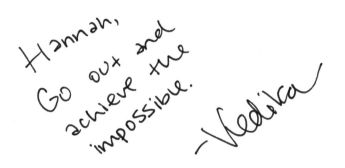

Hannah,
Go out and
achieve the
impossible.
—Vedika

BY VEDIKA DAYAL

*To anyone who has ever felt like their
dreams are out of reach.*

TABLE OF CONTENTS

INTRODUCTION

MAKING SPACE FOR YOUR TOOLKIT

———

Her patronizing tone left my lips pursed and jaw clenched. "You're one girl in a sea of men," she told me, "so don't be disheartened if you don't do well." She gave my body a pointed glance. "And for God's sake, please wear heels."

I was in high school at the time. I had just told my teacher about my decision to participate in a statewide public speaking competition. It wasn't the first time I had been reminded I was short (or a woman). I was 4'10" and hadn't grown an inch since the fifth grade.

You can't do that, it's impossible. It's the universal underdog experience. We are told to be more realistic with our goals, to know our place, to sit down.

Yet nothing makes us want to stand up more.

It's a sentiment passed down for centuries. Roman emperor Marcus Aurelius famously declared that "the impediment to action advances action. What stands in the way becomes the way."[1] The same obstacles that make us the underdog can help us find success. Albert Einstein claimed that "in the middle of every difficulty lies opportunity."[2] Adversity gives us a reason to create. Even Oprah encourages us to turn our wounds into wisdom.[3] The things that cause us the most grief also provide the strongest foundation for our success.

Despite all of this, there is a key piece missing: *how?*

In the media, the "how" is often portrayed as a combination of hard work and luck. They say to work hard and good things will happen, but millions of people still fail to achieve their dreams due to factors beyond their control, like poverty or a lack of opportunity. The Oprahs and Albert Einsteins of the world are few and far between. Is *anything* in our hands?

* * *

My high school was situated in a majority immigrant district. The pressure was high to be successful and to make our parents' sacrifices in coming to a new country worth it. Many of us had been reading college admissions books for fun since the fourth grade. If you studied for your algebra exam at homecoming, you weren't a nerd. You were normal.

As a result, our students did well in everything from tennis to debate to business strategy. The public speaking competition was a rare exception. We sent our best speakers every year and always managed to come back empty-handed. So, when I decided to compete, my teacher wasn't the only one who was skeptical. "No offense, but you don't look the part," one person told me with a shrug.

I had never given a speech before. I prepared the only way I knew how: through brute force. I wrote and rewrote my speech, practicing it out loud every day until my voice was hoarse.

The night before the competition, I had a stare-off with my reflection in the mirror. I met my gaze and told myself that being short was a superpower.

I wore flats and placed first.

There is a myth we have all been told about being an underdog: we need to *overcome* our disadvantages to be successful. To start a company that helps millions of people or use our voice to enact change, we have to succeed *against* the odds. We have to persevere.

After my public speaking escapade, I began wondering if this was true. Before the competition, I'd never been a strong speaker despite trying many times to get better at the craft. I did well because my teacher's words had fueled me instead of discouraged me. In a space where I knew nothing, being the underdog had given me the fire to be bold.

But how could I know it wasn't all a fluke? This question lurked in the back of my mind. What if luck had graced me this one time and would never come back? It seemed likely. After all, I was shy and a pretty average speaker. But as other opportunities to prove myself popped up, I wanted to figure out if I could get lucky again. This book is a product of the journey I went on to find answers.

So, can we be intentional about using our disadvantages to find success? Let's start by looking at the word "underdog."

★ ★ ★

In 43 AD, the Romans invaded Britain. Both sides brought gleaming swords, raging spirits, and fighting dogs to the battlefield. The war instilled a fascination for fighting dogs in the

Romans. In the years that followed, large audiences would gather in the Roman Colosseum to watch gladiator dogs pitted against other animals, such as wild elephants.[4]

The practice retained its popularity until the nineteenth century. When the cost of large animals began to rise, people turned to dog-on-dog combat. It was then the word *underdog* was created to define the dog who lost the fight. Its rival, the expected winner, was called the top dog.[5]

It's been a few centuries since. In most countries, society has evolved past dogfighting. Along with society, the word "underdog" itself has evolved to mean the entity most likely to lose. Often, that entity is no longer a dog trying to battle another dog, but a person trying to battle something more abstract—like stigma, discrimination, or someone else's expectations.

As a society, we celebrate these people. We are drawn to competitions where there are disparities of power, and we cheer on the most disadvantaged person, the fated loser. In psychology, this pattern is called the "underdog effect."[6] It's somewhat paradoxical—we root for the underdog, but no one likes rooting for a loser. So, why do we do it?

Psychologists suggest it's because we all feel like underdogs sometimes. When they succeed despite the odds, we feel hope we too can succeed. While not everyone identifies with the term "underdog," struggle is inherent to the human experience. If you picked up this book and have made it this far, I'd venture to say you've felt like your dreams were out of reach before.

But can our struggles truly be the *reason* for our success?

After winning the public speaking competition, I had many opportunities I didn't take advantage of because I wasn't confident enough. I resorted back to that old myth of underdog perseverance. In order to succeed, I thought I had to find a way to overcome being short: maybe a pair of stilettos would help, or some skin-colored stilts. I thought I had to persevere.

But a coffee chain found on and around street corners throughout the world begs to differ.

* * *

In 2000, Starbucks expanded rapidly across Australia. By 2008, the company had opened about ninety locations in the country. Then, the coffee giant was forced to close more than 70 percent of its stores.[7] What happened?

Let's zoom out. In the mid-1900s, there was an influx of Italian and Greek immigrants to Australia. With them, they brought their love for espresso. It's not just my caffeine-addict bias shining through when I say it was a huge cultural win for Australia. As historian Andrew May explains, espresso coffee was the country's "key watershed between a drab past and a cosmopolitan present."[8]

Espresso bars gave a place for Australian bohemians and teenagers to socialize. As Australian culture grew around coffee, it began to appeal to the broader public. Free from the centuries-long traditions of European countries, Australia was able to explore coffee and make it its own. All across the country, barista competitions and coffee-making classes popped up.[9]

Back to Starbucks: in 2000, Starbucks was the antithesis of the underdog. It had experienced success in Japan, the UK, and the Philippines on top of its explosive growth in North America. It seemed like it was made to be: Australians loved coffee, and Starbucks had loads of it. Starbucks in Australia was the top dog we all envy.

But Australians didn't care much for the American chain. They had their beloved local shops, where the coffee was better and cheaper. While Americans visiting Australia were able to keep Starbucks shops in tourist destinations afloat, other stores were forced to close. When describing the issue, one analyst suggested Starbucks launched too rapidly. It didn't give Australian consumers the chance to develop an appetite for the Starbucks brand.[10] Having a perceived advantage was the root of Starbucks' confidence, but it was also the root of its failure.

Let's fast-forward a few years to Starbucks' expansion to China. In China, where tea culture is intricately tied to the country's history, the coffee chain was a true underdog. But the Starbucks team was aware of the disadvantage and crafted its strategy carefully. Instead of rapidly expanding across the country, the team strategically positioned a couple of stores in high-visibility areas. And instead of loudly promoting its coffee and risking ostracizing itself from Chinese culture, the team curated a menu using local tea ingredients.

They knew they couldn't please everyone and they couldn't transform China into a coffee-loving place overnight. So, they focused on the people they could please: China's emerging middle class.

The new middle class was living in large, rapidly expanding urban hotspots. Many of them were working for American companies and aspired to adopt Western cultural standards. They subscribed to a life of luxury and saw purchasing expensive things as a sign of their elevated quality of life.[11] The Starbucks brand was perceived as distinctly American and exclusive with its pricier-than-average coffee—it was the match made in heaven Starbucks-Australia never could have been.

As of August 2020, Starbucks has more than 4,300 stores in mainland China.[12] The company's growth in the country is overwhelming. While having an apparent advantage hurt Starbucks' chances of success in Australia, the team's disadvantage forced them to think creatively in China. At the root of their success was innovation.

But what was at the root of their innovation?

* * *

The expression "think outside the box" comes from management consultants and their clients hunching over the infamous nine dots puzzle in the 1970s and 1980s.[13]

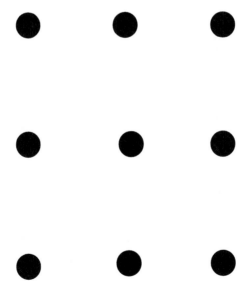

The challenge of the puzzle is to connect all the dots with only four lines. You cannot lift your pen. Try it for a few minutes, then peek at the solution on the next page.

It's frustratingly simple, but very few people actually get to the answer. This is because we perceive an imaginary box around the nine dots we cannot cross; however, these boundaries are entirely in our minds. To solve the puzzle, you have to think outside that box, hence the now-clichéd phrase. The box is not an arbitrary constraint—the shape of the dots gives our solution a structure and a starting place.

Being an underdog is a similar experience. The "box" represents the perceived odds of your success happening. It could be imposed by societal expectations for someone like you or what investors think you should be doing or even what traditional wisdom has to say about your life decisions.

As with the nine dots puzzle, the box is not an insurmountable wall when you're an underdog. Understanding the existence of the imaginary box is key to thinking beyond it and solving the puzzle. Similarly, understanding your disadvantages is key to using them as stepping stones on your journey. All success requires is a bit of innovation to think outside the odds.

Starbucks' innovation stemmed from using its perceived disadvantage (Chinese people's affiliation for tea) in a new way (curating a menu from local tea ingredients). Starbucks' innovation stemmed from being the underdog.

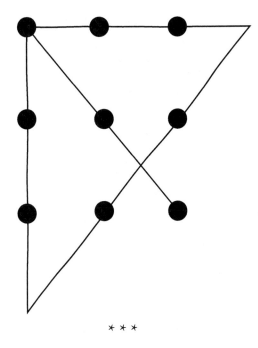

* * *

Your memories may not all be real.

In one study, psychologists asked people about their views on the legalization of marijuana twice: once in 1973 and another time in 1982. In 1982, the people who declared they were against legalization were more likely to recall they were also against it in 1973—even if it wasn't actually true.[14] Our memories are fallible, and often biased by our current values.

This phenomenon is why, when famous people are asked for advice, they resort to platitudes. It's no fault of their own—it's just been too long since they had to chase success. Their memory is now tainted by their own values. The celebrity who values hard work remembers her journey as one of grit. She forgets how crucial her personal network was, or luck. *Work hard,* she says. When dealing with imminent challenges, such platitudes make us feel good. But they don't concretely help us.

While there is a place for books documenting the success of the most famous people in the world, this book isn't one of them. When I set out on this journey, my goal was to learn to channel the energy of that girl-turned-public-speaker from high school. I wanted actionable insights, so I sought out everyday innovators: people who are still growing and remember the time not too long ago when they were struggling to build something new. The kind of people who are less prone to hindsight bias.

I talked to people who nearly flunked out of high school or never had a formal education at all. I talked to people who sold their companies for millions to Apple, LinkedIn, and Squarespace. I talked to people deemed the most creative in the world by *Fast Company*. I talked to founders and creators, inventors and investors.

There are thirteen stories in this book. Each of the thirteen people featured comes from a diverse background, but they all began as underdogs in the space they now thrive in. They all have inspired me in some way. I have no doubt they will do the same for you.

Their innovations were unplanned surprises, but each of them was particularly intentional about three key areas: their environment, their conversations, and their movement through life. Having that intentionality is what allowed them to be innovative when the time called for it. Ultimately, it allowed them to thrive as underdogs. Each section of this book delves into one of the three areas.

The first section of the book is called "Intentional Environment." Environment is a broad term, encompassing everything from our bedroom to our hometown to the context of our social existence. The section explores how we can interact with these different environments in order to foster innovation. When thought about deliberately, even the worst parts of our environment can give us fuel to create.

The second section of the book is called "Intentional Conversation." From listening to speaking to our overall aura, there are many dimensions to how we communicate with people. For the entrepreneurs I spoke with, each dimension was a tool to help them build new things. Conversation is where our underdog nature sticks out the most, which is why it is also our biggest source of leverage.

The last section of the book is called "Intentional Movement." It is less about our physical movement and more about our movement through various stages of life. For many people, lack of opportunity is their biggest barrier to innovation. This section explores how we can seek and experience opportunities more intentionally.

If you are looking to spark creativity in your life, build something new, or change the world in your own little way, this book is here to help you. Each section features four to five stories of innovators as well as research, data, and supplementary stories to give you a thorough look at an underdog principle. Each chapter ends with actionable steps you can take right now to make a concrete change in your life.

This book is an underdog's toolkit for achieving the impossible. Like any toolkit, it is packed with tools to help you approach the problems you're dealing with. And, like any toolkit, you need to make space for it before you bring it into your home. You need to be open-minded to its potential before you try to learn all the information inside.

To make this space for your new toolkit, be ready to embrace being the underdog. Be receptive to disadvantages being the same things setting you apart from your competition. Choose to see low expectations as opportunities to surprise and delight people. Know that as the underdog, you have an inherent push toward innovation. You just need to learn to harness it.

I know you can do it because I'm doing it right now. I'm a twenty-year-old full-time college student publishing a book. This book is me *thinking outside the odds*.

What would you do if you could think outside the odds?

PART I

INTENTIONAL
ENVIRONMENT

CHAPTER 1

———

PLAY YOUR CARDS

———

The smaller the box, the more creative you get to be.

–UMAIMAH MENDHRO

"It was just not in the cards." Seven words that make me seethe through clenched teeth.

You didn't get accepted into your dream school? *Poor thing, it was just not in the cards.* Your project failed to get funding? *I guess your cards have different plans for you.* As a society, we lean on the concept that some things are predestined. It is comforting to think we can't control everything, that there is a force larger than us which ultimately decides our success, whether it's God or the cursed stack of cards we've somehow ended up with.

The thing is, good gamblers don't need good cards to win.

In one research study, scientists dug through over 400 million online poker games played over the course of a year. The research team had one question: was player performance consistent?

The short answer: yes. Players who did well in the first half of the year were up to twelve times more likely to do well in the second half of the year. The players who started off the year doing poorly hardly ever rose to the top. You can't predict the cards a player will get, but you can easily predict their performance. Good gamblers are the ones who know how to play their cards right, whatever a game tosses at them.[15]

Player performance is predictable, but the cards you are dealt are entirely random. Clearly, some players are just better at playing their cards than others.

In another world, Umaimah Mendhro could have been a darn good gambler.

She was born in 1978 in Akri, a village in Pakistan so far from the city center it never made it onto the map. It was not a good time to be a woman in Pakistan. Ten days after Umaimah was born, General Muhammad Zia-ul-Haq seized power and declared martial law in the country. He suspended all fundamental rights guaranteed to women and actively promoted their seclusion from society. "It was the sort of place where I couldn't go out on the street," Umaimah told me.

There was no clean drinking water or proper toilets in Akri. The closest school was dozens of miles away from Umaimah's home. Her parents wanted to educate both her brother and her, but formal education wasn't an option if they stayed in the village. "We'll move to the city," they resolved.

There was just one problem.

Umaimah's parents were doctors, the only ones in the village. Together, the two had built the first hospital in the area. Some of their patients would travel for an entire day on foot to see them. When the patients learned the Mendhros were thinking of leaving, they became desperate. "Please don't leave us," they begged. "We have nowhere else to go."

They were right. There really was nowhere else to go. Umaimah's parents were advocates for education. They had big dreams for their children, ones that extended past this small village with dirt roads leading to nowhere. But they couldn't pursue those dreams at the cost of hundreds of families' healthcare. Their children's education would have to wait.

"We will pray that your kids go to the best school in the world," the people of the community vowed. But with no institutions in sight, the best school felt worlds away. And when Umaimah turned two, it only seemed to become more distant. Zia-ul-Haq had instituted a military regime. Liberal doctors were one target.

Her parents were left with no choice but to flee the country. It's the first memory Umaimah can recall: deafening thumps, then shrieks, and then a breathless escape for survival. The family lived in exile in Saudi Arabia for ten years before they were able to return home to Akri. With all the moving back and forth, Umaimah's education was in disarray. It was as if the dealer of her life had dropped her cards mid-shuffle.

The dealer hands out cards at the beginning of each poker game. Regardless of how skilled you are, you have no control over the ones you receive. Life deals your cards in the form of your environment. You have no choice over the context you grow up in. It's a consequential piece of luck that influences your most treasured perceptions and ideas.

What do you do if you end up with bad cards? Let's take another peek into the world of poker to see how they do it in the big leagues.

* * *

Skill is crucial in poker, but this isn't immediately clear when you play. In fact, for the first couple of rounds, skilled and unskilled players are indistinguishable. On average, the difference becomes clear only after 1,471 hands have been played.[16] It's a tipping point, a crossroads when skill begins to dominate luck.[17]

One thousand four hundred seventy-one. It's a big number. In real-life poker, the wait for skill to matter is likely much longer. "In the long run, there's no luck in poker," one professional describes, "but the short run is longer than most people know." When the short run is long and you're luckless, there is only one way to win: you wait.

Patience is a virtue in most aspects of life, but it's particularly important in poker. When you know you have good cards, it's tempting to bet everything you have and hope luck is on your side. Johnny Moss always did the opposite. The first winner of the Poker World Series would spend the beginning of a game doing the bare minimum he could to survive. When his opponent relaxed, Moss grew fiercer with his strategies, earning him the win.[18] Sometimes, success is about skill. Sometimes, it's just about waiting long enough.

So Umaimah waited.

"What was your most vivid memory of growing up?" I asked her. It's a question I asked everyone I interviewed. I had heard many answers, from their experience learning to skateboard to their first trip abroad.

"I remember we used to walk in the house," Umaimah told me. "My mom and I, back and forth, back and forth, back and forth."

The walks were mellow. "Imagine if I got a really great education," Umaimah would say. A few seconds later would come her mother's response. "We'll figure something out."

The two were pacing and dreaming and waiting. But Umaimah was also often bored. She couldn't go to school, so the only thing she had to do was take annual government-mandated exams. The study material was simple enough that she just needed three to four months to learn it. This brought her to the question: "The rest of the year, what was I supposed to do?"

Many of the people in Akri made their entire incomes from crafts. As Umaimah observed their work from afar, she learned too. "In some ways, the confinement, but also the freedom of space and time, gave me the opportunity to explore," she reflected. She taught herself how to cut and sketch, sew and stitch, print and paint, and create.

Her years of self-directed studying and exploration passed by sluggishly like this. Soon, Umaimah was ready for college.

* * *

In 1963, four men were getting ready for a concert. "What do you all see in your own future?" a reporter asked them. "How long might your fame last?"

"We're lucky if we last three months," one said.

"Who knows. At forty, we may not know how to write songs anymore," another chimed in.

"I hope to have enough money to go into a business of my own by the time we, umm, do 'flop.'"

"I've always fancied having a ladies' hairdressing salon." *Laughter.*[19]

Four men who had no idea what they were talking about.

When my family immigrated from India to the US, they brought two kinds of music with them: Bollywood and The Beatles. As they settled into a strange new world, they sang about women named Jane and streets called Penny Lane. But back in 1963, as the group members were making each other laugh, The Beatles had no way of knowing how fondly their tunes would be remembered by the world.

Back in the 1960s, when The Beatles were first starting out, the band wanted access to the thriving South London music scene. But the four members were teenagers from Liverpool, England, a relatively poor northwest port city. There were no musical venues or professional studios in the area, so The Beatles turned to pubs, crawling through the area to find any dingy place that would let them perform for the night. It was in these cramped spaces they learned about each other's love for hairdressing and dreams for the future. As co-lead vocalist and bassist Paul McCartney later reflected, it was crucial in helping them cement their friendship.[20]

The Beatles' scrappy start had other perks too. Because they didn't have fancy tools, they were forced to compromise with creativity. The resulting music felt relatable while being incredibly complex.[21] By using their lack of resources as a driver for innovation, the group was successfully playing their cards.

Umaimah, too, was learning how to play her cards. Her high exam scores qualified her for one of the best universities in Pakistan. Still, she found herself wanting more. The university only had two majors, neither of which she was particularly interested in. It was not a welcoming place. "I felt very aware of gender," she recalled, "the differences in how men and women are treated." She wanted to go to school somewhere else. She wanted to go to school in America.

Her parents were unsure about letting her go to a new country on her own as a woman. Her brother was studying there at Purdue University. "What if I went to Purdue with him?" she asked. They relented. It was the only university they let her apply to.

"My parents are very liberal," Umaimah told me. "They're very supportive, so it's interesting that there was still this thing..." she trailed off. There was still this thing that her life was dependent on men.

Umaimah was accepted into Purdue and came to America for school in 2001. America was a whole new world. "The fountain drinks are humongous," she told me laughingly. But there were bigger differences too. "I had never been in a real classroom like that. I could have my peers look over an essay or debate with them for hours."

After college, Umaimah worked at Microsoft as a product manager. She was there for four years, before being accepted into Harvard Business School. Her village's vows were coming to fruition.

But Umaimah felt uncomfortable studying at one of the best universities in the world. "I'm at Harvard, and my cousins back home don't even know how to spell 'Harvard,'" she said. "It's the same gene pool. I'm not an exceptionally smart person compared to them. I felt guilty, but it was more like I needed to do something about it."

When you're in an environment that is more plentiful than you're used to, it has a certain novelty to it. With that novelty, you're better able to appreciate its intricacies. With that heightened appreciation, you're primed for innovation. It's a lesson The Beatles had discovered many years ago.

As the group began getting attention, they got access to a professional recording studio on a pretty little street called Abbey Road. It was a novel place to them, extraordinary in its abundance. It had all the shiny hardwood floors and grand pianos they could want. The Beatles understood how special their newfound tools were, so they were relentless in finding new ways to innovate with them. To a new listener, their albums might sound like the product of many different artists—every song used instruments and technology in a distinct way. Music theorists now credit The Beatles' experimentation with revolutionizing the recording process.[22]

Many years later, The Beatles decided to stop making music together. Their last album was their most famous one. They called it *Abbey Road.*

When you've fought to be in an environment, that place means something more to you. You want to make the most of it. Umaimah had yet to figure out how she could make the most of her experience at Harvard. She remembered one of her childhood dreams of being an artist. *Maybe I could use art to change the world*, she thought. But she quickly found it was nearly impossible to make a living off creative work. Success in art was reserved for an elite few and she wasn't one of them.

In some ways, she felt like she was destined to fail, like her urge to innovate would remain forever a dream. Her struggle begged the question: why was it so hard?

✶ ✶ ✶

Everything happens for a reason. While it's a comforting thought, it's hard to rationalize in practice. We are often given circumstances that make it hard to find the silver lining. But even if everything can't happen for a clear reason, you can give everything a reason.

Umaimah had been given many cards. She had grown up secluded from the rest of the world, so she had taught herself various crafts. She was raised in Pakistan, where she observed the lives of people who struggled to make ends meet. She was intimately familiar with technology, as she'd studied computer science in college. To win the game, your cards have to work together. Umaimah was playing to win, so VIDA was born.

VIDA is an e-commerce platform Umaimah founded in 2014. The word *vida* means "a rare find" in Persian, "beloved" in Hebrew, "life" in Spanish, and "wisdom" in Sanskrit. The word is as universal as the brand Umaimah wanted to create. Paris had incredible artists, but so did Akri, Mumbai, and Tokyo. She wanted to tell the stories of creatives everywhere.

At the time, the big things happening in the technology industry hadn't reached fashion, but she saw the industry needed innovation desperately. Makers and designers were siloed from each other. Brands bridged that gap, but they also profited off the disconnect. Umaimah wanted to shuffle the system around so everyone benefited equally.

VIDA allows artists around the world to upload their designs and have them printed on responsibly made apparel and accessories. The fun is not reserved for digital artists either—photographers, sculptors, and calligraphers can all put their work on the platform.

From her roots in Pakistan to her love for art to her experience in technology, VIDA brings all of Umaimah's environments together. With her understanding of technology, she can print onto materials other companies shy from, like leather and metal. She explores 3D printing with 3D knitting and 3D molds for jewelry. All items are made to order, so the company's capital is never stuck in inventory. Umaimah funnels that extra money in the bank into education and empowerment programs for her designers and factory workers.

In today's innovation ecosystem, big companies have a disproportionate amount of power. When they see start-ups that could threaten their power, they recreate the start-ups' offerings. They crush competition. If you don't want to be trapped in their iron grip, you have to create something that cannot be copied.

Luckily, you have a set of circumstances no one else can lay claim to. "When you use your history, your gender, your ethnicity, your disabilities, you can craft a future that only you can for the world," Umaimah says. To create something that cannot be copied, to win this innovation poker game, all you have to do is play your cards.

Winning hands take the spoils in poker. How can you get yours?

THE DISAPPEARING DISADVANTAGE

My first time walking into a preschool as an adult, my 4'10 body seemed huge.

I awkwardly crouched down onto one of the tiny chairs. The children running around me were small relative to the rest of the human world, but the furniture was made to match their size. It created an environment where their biggest disadvantage—size—disappeared. It wasn't an insignificant factor either: small furniture has been proven to be crucial for children's development.[23]

Snack bars helped Daniel Lubetzky discover an environment where his disadvantage also disappeared. He is an entrepreneur from Mexico with European heritage of Jewish faith who lives in America. In other words, he is every labeler's worst nightmare.

As a kid, he tried to be friends with *everyone*. He knew how to say "hello, how are you?" in at least forty languages. Some would call it weirdly obsessive, while others would say he's a natural connector.

They would both be partially wrong.

Lubetzky's father was a Holocaust survivor, so Lubetzky was very aware of his own mortality. "There was an existential aspect of trying to connect with people," he described. He wanted to make sure if there was ever a war, he would be able to survive.[24] He was terrified of failure; yet, as he grew older, one of the most failure-prone life paths captured his attention.

He realized snack bars *sucked*. They were either "very indulgent and just full of sugar or they tasted like cardboard or like plastic." He wanted to become an entrepreneur and create his own snack bar, one with ingredients you could actually pronounce. It would be under a company called KIND. The problem? He lived in a world where no one else shared his vision. People didn't even want *remotely* healthy snack bars. "Bars are meant to be unhealthy," they told him, rolling their eyes. "That's the whole point." It felt like KIND was destined to fail.[25]

But what was larger than Lubetzky's fear of failure was his belief in KIND. In 1994, Lubetzky went to his first trade show. As he later reflected, these trade shows were literally a matter of survival: he had to make enough sales to cover the cost of attending the show and paying his team. He was ready to do anything to stop the people walking briskly past his booth long enough for a sample.[26]

Lubetzky was forcing his survival instinct to kick in.

When you ask Google what makes a good salesman, the top results all mention a lack of desperation. One even boldly claims that "desperation is one trait that never looks good on anyone." Full stop.

But desperation breeds hunger and hunger breeds hustle. When every interaction means the world to you, you'll do anything you can to make things click. And for Lubetzky, they began clicking. Soon, he moved beyond trade shows to travel—he offered anyone from a bored consultant in the waiting area to whoever happened to be sitting next to him on his flight a free bar.

Lubetzky's success came from these little interactions, his unique ability to connect with people. Once people tried his bars, they became like ambassadors, encouraging their friends to go buy the bars. KIND was that good. Word of mouth made it a billion-dollar snack company.

The environments we grow up in can equip us with crippling weaknesses, but a weakness in one environment isn't always a weakness in another. A fear of failure is a weakness in a start-up accelerator, but it is an asset at trade shows. A perfectionist tendency is a bad card in a fast-paced environment, but it is a good card in a slower one. The Disappearing Disadvantage Method is about seeking out the environments where your disadvantages are no longer such.

But what if you're dealing with a disadvantage that cannot disappear?

BE THE BIG FISH

Language-learning app Duolingo was founded in Pittsburgh in 2011 by Luis von Ahn. At the time, the city was lacking as a tech center, especially compared to the likes of Silicon Valley. The talent pool was close to zero. Von Ahn wanted to attract technical employees, but how?

The big-fish-little-pond effect highlights that our perception of ourselves is dependent on the people around us. The little fish in the big pond can enjoy the vastness of her home and the company of many other little fishes, but she will always have to try harder to be seen. The big fish in the little pond has to squeeze her fins together to fit, but she will always feel confident in her grandeur.

The Duolingo team found themselves in a city with very few people in their industry, so they decided to embrace being the big fish. They placed billboards around San Francisco that read "Own a home. Work in tech. Move to Pittsburgh."[27] The message was simple and effective to employees who were used to apartments with sky-high rents. Pittsburgh stood out.

After attracting workers to Duolingo, von Ahn experienced lower churn rates than companies in more prominent cities.[28] He attributes this to the lack of other competing tech opportunities in the city.[29] By being one of a few, Duolingo was able to be the best option: the big shiny fish in the cramped pond. When your environment itself is the underdog, there is more room for you to innovate. The seeming lack of opportunity *is* the opportunity.

If all this is making you skeptical, you're not alone. We live in a society that rejects small ponds. From the moment we're old enough to understand the question "so, what do you want to do when you're older?" we're told to think big—to get into the best school, work at the best company, and be in the best industry. With so many opportunities in big ponds, what's the point of a small pond?

On a Thursday, I video-called one of the most well-networked women in the world for answers. Jesse Draper had agreed to squeeze me between two crucial meetings that day. I had just fifteen minutes to understand the merits of the small pond.

Draper uses her leverage to advocate for women by investing in their companies. Her firm, Halogen Ventures, has had dozens of successful investments in companies acquired by giants like Walmart and Twitter. While there is no shortage of female founder talent, she told me, her job is far from smooth.[30] There are too many women who have to heave and sweat to get funding and not enough people willing to give it to them. When she tries to secure investors in her fund, they scoff. "There aren't enough good female-founded companies out there for this to be profitable," they say. "I'm not in venture for community service."

"Investing in women is not a charity," she wants to scream until her words finally sink to the bottom of her prospect's brain. Instead, she takes a deep breath and moves on to the next.

It's a consequential choice. One of the founders Draper invested in started a menstruation brand with proprietary technology in a billion-dollar market. When the founder sought more funding, she had to present to room after room of people who had never experienced menstruation. It was like pushing a car uphill. "What kind of start-up wants to fix menstruation?" they asked her. She saw her bank account hit zero. Her co-founder left. She wondered if it was a sign to quit.

Half the world is women. Yet, in the health industry, only 3 percent of funding goes to women's health start-ups. To survive in such a small pond, Draper's founder had to stretch every dollar she got, making sure all 100 cents were put to work. She persisted. "Now, she's doing incredible," Draper told me. "She just blows things out of the water."

To play your cards, sometimes you have to squeeze your fins together. While starting a company in a taboo industry makes it harder to get funding, it can also help you optimize the money you do get. While growing up in a village with no schools can make it hard to learn, it can also make your story stand out amongst a pile of otherwise similar applications. Being the big fish makes it harder to survive, but if you do, it becomes just a bit easier to innovate.

✳ ✳ ✳

Let's get back to VIDA. The company grew rapidly, and Umaimah realized she would need funding from investors to sustain the growth. Her first pitch was to Google Ventures in 2014. A few weeks later, they offered her a check for $1 million.

It's a rare event in the start-up world, but Umaimah had been waiting for thirty-six years. Her short run was finally over. It was the tipping point in the game where skill began to take over.

Another one of VIDA's first investors? Jesse Draper.

As of 2021, VIDA has worked with some of the biggest forces in pop culture, including Cher, the Golden Globes, Steve Madden, and Warner Bros. The company has been cited as one of Fast Company's "World-Changing Ideas" and has empowered hundreds of small artists around the world. Many of these artists have grown up in environments with less opportunity and thus often struggled to make ends meet. VIDA has been the secret to their strategies for winning their own poker games.

There is a famous poker story often told with big grins and wide eyes in casinos everywhere. It is a story of Moss and the world's most famous gambler, Nick "The Greek" Dandalos. Moss had a close friend named Benny Binion, who owned a casino. In 1949, Dandalos trudged in looking to play a good game of poker. Binion knew just the person who would make a worthy opponent. Binion called Moss.

The Dandalos-Moss match lasted five months.

Legend has it Moss beat Dandalos out of $4 million dollars before Dandalos finally stood up from the table to quit. "Mr. Moss," he said, "I have to let you go."[31] It is likely the most famous line in poker history.

It's contested among historians if this match ever actually happened. But whether your opponent is the most famous gambler in the world or a series of unfortunate circumstances, if you play your cards right, one day your opponent too will sigh in frustration and let you go.

The spoils will be yours.

PLAY YOUR CARDS

- Life gives you a set of circumstances that only you can have. If you create with them in mind, your work will be unique by default.

- Characteristics you perceive as weaknesses may be strengths in a different environment. Write down your shortcomings and disadvantages. Where can they be an asset to you? What kind of environment would need a trait like that?

- Standing out in a place where everyone is doing what you're doing is hard. Standing out in a place where no one is doing anything is easier. If your environment doesn't have many opportunities, embrace that as a way to stand out.

CHAPTER 2

WHERE THE FRONTIER LIES

———

When in doubt, I would err on the side of exploring.

—DANIEL GROSS

When Neil Armstrong stepped on the moon in 1969, people's eyes probably lit up as they dreamed of the twenty-first century. Orbiting space hotels. Antigravity theme parks. Friendship bracelets exchanged with extraterrestrial life on Mars. The possibilities were endless.

But to Elon Musk in 2001, that world still seemed like a distant dream. When he went to NASA's website, he couldn't even find anything about Mars. NASA had no plans to send anyone to the Red Planet—or even back to the moon. *How could this be possible?*

Out of his bewilderment, Musk's company, SpaceX was born.

When he told people about his plans to build a space company, one friend made him watch a graphic video of rockets blowing up. Others tutted, predicting he was going to lose money. The only people who dabbled in space were large government agencies that had been around for decades, they told him.[32]

On May 30, 2020, NASA astronauts successfully took off for the International Space Station from American soil. It was the first time this had ever happened in a commercially built and operated American-manned spacecraft. The rocket was made by SpaceX.[33] How did someone with no aerospace background end up pushing the frontier of rocket science?

And what on earth is a frontier?

* * *

Rockets are made of materials like aluminum, titanium, and copper. Let's say you gather all the materials needed for a very basic rocket ship. You stack them on the floor in their appropriate quantities and wave a magic wand so the pieces fall together into rocket ship formation. What would it cost?

Musk calculated it would cost $500,000. But at the time, the price for such a basic rocket ship was *$25 million*, fifty times more than the cost of its raw materials. NASA had no plans to go to Mars because rocket ships were so expensive. People wanted to go to the planet, but they weren't ready to give up millions of dollars for it.

Musk realized the issue lay in "how the atoms are arranged." The formation of rocket ships from raw materials wasn't as efficient as it could be. His goal with SpaceX was to reduce the cost of putting together the raw materials.[34]

As of 2019, NASA would pay $90 million to fly with Boeing, the leading competitor, and $55 million to fly with SpaceX.[35]

The SpaceX team managed to cut down the cost of a rocket ship by 40 percent.[36]

So, what's the secret?

A frontier is defined as the extreme limit of understanding or achievement in a particular area. Progress is enabled by challenging those current boundaries of knowledge, by pushing on what we already know into the unknown.

A small fraction of 1 percent of people in the world have gone to space. It is a field where our knowledge is still limited, and SpaceX is operating at our knowledge's greatest extent. In a place where only a few legacy players dare to wander, the SpaceX team is the underdog. Being new to the field, they bring the freshest perspective on innovation.[37] Their perspective is what allows them to thrive.

In other words, the frontier rewards misfits. While more established spaces shy from new ways of thinking, you have to explore to survive on the frontier. The frontier rewards the underdog.

The problem? Finding frontiers. It can feel like innovators like Musk are destined to be on grand frontiers while the rest of us are doomed to the middle of conformity. After all, not everyone is looking to radically advance humanity.

Are there environments where we can find everyday frontiers? I went to a young Israeli founder for some answers.

✳ ✳ ✳

Daniel Gross grew up in Jerusalem, Israel, where he often felt like an outsider looking in. "High school wasn't interesting," he told me. "I didn't have many friends. And I didn't have much to be passionate about."

It was the early 2000s. Technology was changing life for many rapidly. While Israel has the most start-ups per capita of anywhere in the world, a lot of that innovation happens in the bustling heart of Tel Aviv. In contrast, Daniel found the ancient city of Jerusalem to be "more offline than online."

So, Daniel turned to the digital world for inspiration. He hung out in online technology forums, played video games, and taught himself to code. Coding was doubly beneficial—it fostered his love for technology and let him hack video games so he could win.

"What did you want to be when you grew up?" I asked him. A software engineer? A professional hacker? A CEO?

"I had no clue," he admitted. "And it was terrifying." The kids around him were laser-focused and knew exactly what they wanted to do with their careers. All Daniel knew was that he loved to build things for people.

After graduating high school, Daniel went to government-mandated military camp. Around the same time, there were whispers online about a small Silicon Valley company called Y Combinator.[38] YC was a start-up accelerator and rumor had it the program culminated with a pitch to some of the hottest investors in the area.[39]

YC sounded cool enough to Daniel, so in the middle-of-nowhere-Israel, he connected his trusty Nokia cell phone to a clunky laptop and applied. A few weeks later, he received an invite to come to Silicon Valley. YC called it an "interview." Daniel called it a "chance to see California."

When he stumbled into YC's headquarters, founding partner Paul Graham was not impressed with Daniel's pitch. It wasn't particularly well-developed or interesting. As Graham challenged his idea, staying in Israel was starting to seem like Daniel's destiny.

YC is located on Pioneer Way, an ordinary street where some of the world's most extraordinary companies have been born. As Daniel walked down the street ready for the long journey home, he heard a man behind him, panting to catch up. It was Graham. "Come back in," he puffed out.

Graham didn't like Daniel's idea, but he found the teenager interesting. "How about you come to YC and you can build something new?"

Daniel paused for what felt like an eternity to him.

Before he knew it, he was flying to Israel to pack his suitcase for a three-month trip to California, the duration of the accelerator. He's been living out of that same old suitcase for over a decade now.

* * *

As of 2021, YC is one of the most well-known start-up programs in the world. Billion-dollar companies like Airbnb, DoorDash, and Reddit are all YC alumni.[40] But back when Daniel applied, the program was barely a few years old and the only accelerator of its kind. He had no way of knowing he was on the frontier of something really big that day on Pioneer Way—he merely got lucky.

Luck wasn't always on his side.

After spending months at YC working diligently on his start-up idea, Daniel's cofounder dropped out suddenly in the last two days. He left Daniel with forty-eight hours to build a new company from scratch that he could pitch to the largest investors in Silicon Valley. He left Daniel with forty-eight hours to do three months of work.

That day, Daniel trudged over to Graham's house. "What now?" he asked Graham.

"Just build something that you'd want to use," Graham encouraged.

Daniel did have something he would love to use. It had been at the back of his mind for a while, but it had always seemed too daring. He wanted a search engine for his life.

In 2008, search engines were an entirely novel idea, reserved for technology elites like Google. Daniel was an eighteen-year-old with no formal coding education. "It was like the big frontier technology," he explained to me. "It felt like no one had approved me to do this."

But it was the only idea Daniel had. Having little money of his own, he couldn't stay in California after the program ended, so he decided he had nothing to lose. In the next forty-eight hours, he built a half-broken prototype, bought a domain name, and crossed his fingers.[41]

He called his search engine Greplin. In a few clicks, it would allow you to search through all your information living in various corners of the internet, from Gmail to Facebook. Though his demo was practically nonexistent, the idea caught investors' eyes.

Daniel spent the next few months making his prototype functional. When he finally secured $200,000 in funding, he had just $300 left in the bank. Each time Daniel was on the brink of failure, it was being on the frontier that helped him turn his luck around.

The rapid pace of his success can give you whiplash. Each frontier he found led to a bigger one. A few years after receiving his first investment, Daniel stumbled upon the frontier of machine learning. He pivoted Greplin to Cue, a personal assistant app that turned your emails, contacts, and files into a daily agenda. Three years later, Cue was acquired by Apple. Daniel joined the team as Apple's youngest director of all time.[42]

So, anyone know the directions to the nearest life-changing frontier?

THE FIVE THING RULE

You are 57 percent more likely to become obese if your friend becomes obese. Even if a friend of a friend who you don't know personally becomes obese, you are about 20 percent more likely to gain weight too. This pattern continues for distant connections, many friends of friends out.[43]

The same applies to smoking and even happiness.[44] According to one medical sociology professor at Harvard Medical School, this is because friends affect each other's perceptions of almost everything.[45] They can make us think smoking is okay for our health or feel optimistic about our potential for happiness.

It's why entrepreneur Jim Rohn famously declared, "You are the average of the five people you spend the most time with."[46] The people you are around can change the norms you internalize—they can change your life.

If you needed help right now, who are the five people you would call? Who are the five people each of your people would call? Do they all inspire you to create?

And why does it matter?

Daniel describes the frontier as opaque: it's not always clear what to do next or even if it's worth it to continue. Having the right people around you creates an "internal combustion engine of creativity," he says. It helps you endure uncertainty and stay motivated.

Not everyone has the luxury of surrounding themselves with the right people, but the one place most people can turn to is the internet. There are dozens of corners of the internet where people gather and learn. You don't have to be in physical contact with people to spend time with them.

It doesn't end with people either. You can be the average of the ideas and information you surround yourself with. This is what helped Daniel when he taught himself coding. The same resources that showed him how to hack video games were the ones buzzing about YC in 2008. Your surroundings can inspire you to keep building through uncertainty, but they can also lead you directly toward frontiers.

The Five Thing Rule says you're the average of the five things you spend your most time with. These things can be anything from your family to online forums to media websites to online learning platforms. If your five things inspire you and challenge your ways of thinking about the world, they maximize your chances of finding yourself on the frontier of something new.

How can you ensure your environment does the same?

CREATE POSITIVE FEEDBACK LOOPS

Many entrepreneurial people opt to work at large corporations. While at a start-up, the return on investment is higher if the company explodes, it's hard to know when the start-up is one that will. Corporate opportunities have lower reward, but they also have lower risk.

Still, corporate preference isn't a universal phenomenon. In places like Silicon Valley and Tel Aviv, there are high rates of start-up involvement. Much of the reason for this disparity is entrepreneurs like Kamran Elahian. In the mid-1990s, he would coast through the streets of Silicon Valley in his Ferrari F355, proudly displaying a license plate that read *Momenta*. It was the name of a company he had founded and seen go bankrupt within three years. "I decided to put my biggest failure [on my license plate]," he explained, "That way, I have to be reminded of it every time I get in the car."[47] In a place with people flaunting their failures like trophies, risk seems less *risky*.

So, what creates a culture so accepting of screw-ups in the first place? Three words: positive feedback loops.

Dave McClure, founding partner of a leading Silicon Valley incubator called 500 Startups, calls the firm a fail factory. "We're here trying to 'manufacture fail' on a regular basis, and we think that's how you learn," he explains.[48]

500 Startups is a microcosm of the place it sits in: rewarding new ideas and pouring money into founders it believes in even if they don't ultimately succeed. It's a positive feedback loop that encourages founders who would otherwise shy away from uncertainty to pursue frontiers. In a world where failure is

often talked about in hushed whispers, it encourages founders to embrace their mistakes.

The trick is in finding this environment for ourselves.

Daniel found positive feedback loops at YC, where he had utter freedom to explore different ideas. Even when Graham didn't like his initial pitch, the team was willing to fund Daniel to join the program and explore whatever he wanted. It was a positive feedback loop that minimized risk for a teenager with little money of his own.

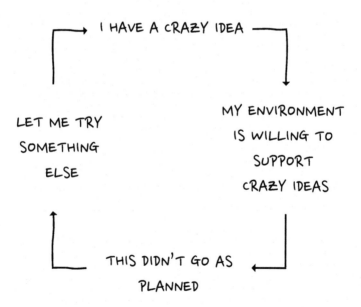

ENVIRONMENTS WITH POSITIVE
FEEDBACK LOOPS HELP YOU
FIND FRONTIERS

I HAVE A CRAZY IDEA

MY ENVIRONMENT
IS WILLING TO
SUPPORT
CRAZY IDEAS

LET ME TRY
SOMETHING
ELSE

THIS DIDN'T GO AS
PLANNED

But everyday innovation doesn't require getting into one of the most selective accelerators in the world. There is potential for small positive feedback loops all around us. If you choose your environment carefully, it should create positive feedback loops for you—inspiring you to pursue the opportunities and ideas that excite you most.

One environment to consider is your workplace. A common example is Google. Google encourages employees to spend 20 percent of their paid work time on side projects that could benefit the company. The 20% Project creates a positive feedback loop by compensating employees for taking creative risks. It's proven to have high returns for Google—it's how Gmail came about.[49] Our inboxes would have looked entirely different if Google didn't create positive feedback loops for its employees.

Finding the right environment will put you a step closer to where the frontier lies—the way you think about closing the gap to the frontier will shape the way you ultimately experience it. "Treat it like playing jazz," Daniel advises. While classical music is carefully planned, jazz is about following what feels right in the moment. It is low-pressure artistry. There is no correct way to play a piece.

In the same way, there is no correct way to lean into positive feedback loops and embrace frontiers. There is no clear end goal to race toward. So, give yourself liberty. Take breaks. Talk yourself through bumps in the road with kindness. Build positive feedback loops.

Play jazz.

✷ ✷ ✷

To Daniel, the most surprising part of his story was how much it meant for someone to believe in him. It allowed him to go from a teenager in Jerusalem who always felt like an outsider to an entrepreneur in Silicon Valley and a director at Apple.

Today, he's trying to create the same experience for hundreds of people around the world with his new company, Pioneer. Pioneer gamifies the experience of innovation through a leaderboard structure that rewards those who complete different tasks for their start-up idea. If you do well in the leaderboard, you get access to industry-leading mentors and funding. It gives users access to a community of people who can inspire them. It creates positive feedback loops for the outsiders who need it most.

"We want to motivate people to become the best versions of themselves, to take their crazy ideas more seriously, and to make betting on themselves less daunting," Pioneer's website says. "If we do what we've set out to, we'll not just fund successful start-ups that might not have otherwise worked out—we'll fund ones that wouldn't have existed at all."[50] For an underdog, successfully finding a frontier and being a pioneer can be the difference between creating something new and never even thinking to try.

Pioneers chart the uncharted and encourage others around them to do the same. How can you find your own frontiers to pioneer?

WHERE THE FRONTIER LIES

- While established spaces shy from new ways of thinking, emerging spaces reward misfits. It is easier for underdogs to innovate and stand out on the frontier.

- Write down the names of the five people you would call if you needed help right now. Who are the five people each of your people would call? Do they all inspire you to create?

- If they do not, write down five other places where you can find inspiration and community. Consider online forums, local entrepreneurship groups, and digital learning platforms.

- Craft your environment so it encourages you to take risk. Consider your workplace, the people around you, your digital home, and the physical place where you live. The positive feedback loops they create will help you feel more comfortable taking risks. That, in turn, will maximize your chance of finding yourself on a frontier.

CHAPTER 3

PRY OPEN THE OYSTER

———

It's okay to be impatient, to not take no for an answer. Get things out into the world, and then iterate.

—AKSHAY KOTHARI

I imagine fishermen probably laugh every time someone cheerfully says, "the world is your oyster." They mean well, but oysters themselves are never the goal—you want pearls. Unfortunately for fishermen and non-fishermen alike, those lustrous pearls are difficult to get to. You have to open up the oyster with gloves on and a special oyster knife, inserting the knife at a specific point of the oyster and twisting carefully before cutting through. Dozens of articles are dedicated to the painstaking process.

The world works in a similar way. While it may very well be your oyster, the journey to the pearls can be a grueling one. And it is true that any place can be your oyster, but you'll only find the pearls inside if you do the work needed to pry it open.

So, what's the trick?

* * *

If you happened to be at a particular Japanese supermarket in Palo Alto in 2009 enjoying a hot bowl of ramen noodles, you might have found a young man with glasses observing your slurping and then rapidly writing something in his notebook. His name was Akshay Kothari. He is one person who sees pearls wherever he goes.

Akshay was a grad student at Stanford at the time of his ramen-watching spree. It was part of an assignment he had for a class on design thinking: redesign the way people ate ramen noodles.

While many years later, the world still eats ramen in the same sloppy way, Akshay was changed by the experience. After spending hours watching people at the local supermarket and noting the inefficiencies of the process, he began thinking about empathy and its role in innovation—to build good products, you have to intimately understand the user's challenges first.

During his two years at Stanford, Akshay went through five failed start-ups. I sat down with him for an interview and asked him the question anyone would after hearing about five consecutive failures: "Why did you keep going?"

"It was Silicon Valley," Akshay answered with a smile. "Entrepreneurship was in the air." He found the energy infectious and start-ups thrilling.

But there's an art to letting that energy permeate through you, to seizing the pearls of your environment. Most people in the Valley, after all, still work for other people. To be intentional about how you interact with your environment, you have to let its positive energy become yours.

As investor and entrepreneur Paul Graham describes, "Great cities attract ambitious people. You can sense it when you walk around one. In a hundred subtle ways, the city sends you a message."[51] But the message is subtle—you find it in "things you see through windows, in conversations you overhear."[52] Prying open the oyster is about peering into those windows and leaning into those conversations.

Just to get to the design thinking class, Akshay had to pry open many oysters. One of them was Stanford. Stanford is known for being one of the best universities in the world, but as Akshay would find, its pearls are not found by merely fulfilling the requirements of his electrical engineering degree.

As he was walking through campus on his first day, marveling at the architecture, he bumped into a student who worked at the design school. He told Akshay about a boot camp on design thinking at Stanford's d.school.[53] Akshay had never taken a design class in his life. Still, he decided to make a quick detour to check the d.school out.

"It was like being in a candy store," Akshay said, bright-eyed, recounting his first steps into the place.

There were no traditional classroom-style walls, and all the furniture was on wheels, allowing for chairs and tables to be moved around easily and often. He was surrounded by brightly colored Post-its, innovative ideas on whiteboards, and chattering students discussing the future while watching the world go by. There were no doubts left in his mind—he had to sign up for this boot camp.

It was the beginning of his journey through entrepreneurship. There was a large sign hanging outside of the classroom that read, "Nothing is a mistake. There's no win and no fail. There's only make." Throughout his time at Stanford, Akshay tried to internalize that message.

But two years later, Akshay was feeling ready to give up on start-ups. He tried an app that let you send a text message from a series of templates. He tried a website that put all your Facebook data in a visual timeline.[54] He tried a project to help improve nutrition in Rwanda. All his ideas were failing—fast.

It was his last semester. "I almost didn't like start-ups anymore," he admitted to me. "I'd tried a bunch of things that didn't really work and I was going to just join Microsoft after graduation. That was my backup plan."

A job at Microsoft wasn't too shabby of a gig, but were his entrepreneurial dreams still in reach?

✷ ✷ ✷

When Gmail marks your parent's email as spam because it contains links to one too many dating websites, that's a binary classification algorithm at work.[55]

In machine learning, binary classification is when you have two predefined categories. Your goal is to classify items as either one of the categories. Is the email spam or not spam? Is your ice cream good quality or bad quality?

Is the oyster open or not open?

The thing about binary classifiers is that they can be a pain to build. Your code will only tell you the end result: one of the two categories. If it tells you the email is spam when it's not, you have no way of knowing how close it was to being right. It might have been *almost* declared "not spam." Or it might be as far as possible from the truth.

Oysters work in a similar way. When you're knifing carefully through an oyster, it's hard to know if you're doing it correctly. The process is painstaking, and the oyster pops open suddenly. In the moments when you feel like it's not worth it anymore, it might be a sign that you're almost there.

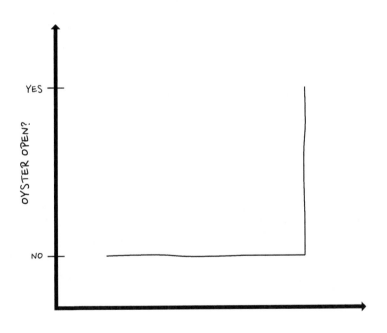

PRYING OPEN AN OYSTER

AMOUNT OF EFFORT

Akshay continued to whittle away at his oyster by signing up for a class called Launchpad, which he took with one of his friends and fellow entrepreneurs, Ankit Gupta. On the first day of class, they were each given a piece of paper to sign. It stated that if you didn't publicly launch a product by the end of the class, you'd fail the course. Akshay scrawled his name on the line.

The pressure to graduate meant Akshay and Ankit had to launch *something*. Still, the question remained: what could it be?

* * *

Neuroscientist Daniel Levitin believes what college professors refuse to believe: our brains have limited capacity. To process all the information we're exposed to everyday, we have to clear some of the existing information, either by storing it away or throwing it out.[56]

Akshay sees his capacity for ideas in a similar way. To make room for new and better ideas, he has to first test out the ones already floating around in his mind. By the time he took Launchpad, he had tested and thrown out many ideas. His mind was primed for new ones.

The iPad had just launched. Ankit and Akshay often worked together in cafés and noticed people increasingly reading the news from their brand-new iPads. There was no efficient way to read news from all your favorite outlets in one place. People were constantly switching between tabs to get all the information they wanted. So, they decided to build an iPad app that aggregated the news. They called it Pulse.

The two didn't have an office nor the means to conduct elaborate market research. This turned out to be one of their biggest, unexpected advantages. "We didn't need to move around at all [to test the app]," Akshay explained to me. "Everybody was sitting in cafés, reading the news already."

Working out of a local café, Ankit would code the app while Akshay would take the iPad around to café-goers to personally get their thoughts on Pulse. The continuous feedback cycle meant they were iterating by the hour, testing whether their work was resonating in real time.

The process from ideation to launch was six weeks. The two submitted the app to the App Store and passed the class.

Soon, it was Akshay's last Monday at Stanford. At the time, Apple had just launched the iPhone 4. Before unveiling the product at Apple's Worldwide Developers Conference, Steve Jobs wanted to highlight some of the other strides the company had made.

Jobs waved his hands around as he scanned the audience. "Let me just show you some of the latest apps that have been out," he said with an offhand gesture at the screen.

Akshay was watching the conference idly from his dorm. He almost toppled off his chair when he processed what was on his screen.

"Pulse is a wonderful RSS reader, if you haven't seen it," Jobs said. He was pointing to a screenshot of Akshay's brainchild.

It violated all the start-up laws out there. Pulse's launch would generally be considered a minimum viable product (MVP), a concept popularized by Eric Ries in *The Lean Startup*.[57] The MVP is a product with the bare minimum of features to launch. It's designed for forgiving early adopters who can give feedback and help iterate the product to perfection. It's not designed for press and attention. But by the time Jobs was showing Pulse, the app had already climbed to the top of the iPad app store and received a feature from the *New York Times*.

On top of Pulse's first iteration being a mere MVP, Akshay was far from a designer. "I didn't know the difference between Serif and Sans Serif yet," he said, laughing.

Clean, aesthetic design is often considered a make-or-break feature for start-ups, and Pulse didn't check the box. "It was rickety at best," Akshay described to me.

What Akshay did have is some knowledge on design thinking from his first semester taking the design thinking class. He was able to craft an app that was user-friendly and interactive based on his knowledge of users, gained from hours of observing café-goers. It was a skill he'd been honing since his early days in graduate school, watching people slurp down their ramen.

Pulse even earned its spot on a few design blogs, just on the ingenious user experience. And as a company that thrived on superior design, Apple's vote of confidence was unprecedented but not unwelcome.

Akshay didn't know it when he was initially taking the design thinking class, but his work helped him eventually pop open the oyster from its hinges. Effort is cumulative, even if it doesn't feel like it's making a difference in the moment.

Three years later, Pulse had gained over thirty million users, and LinkedIn bought the company for ninety million dollars. Pulse's explosive success was far from luck—it was the result of Akshay's consistent drive to seek opportunities and make the most of his environment. Each of his failed attempts at entrepreneurship resulted in a different lesson he was able to apply when building Pulse.

Finding pearls didn't stop after Pulse. Akshay entered LinkedIn as a project manager for the app, but as his cofounder, Ankit, described, he seized opportunities everywhere. He was known to be working simultaneously "on ten different things across sales, products, and engineering." Despite his youth at the time, Akshay's interactions with his environment made him the perfect choice for leading LinkedIn India, the company's second-largest market.[58]

Knowing all this about Akshay's journey and his successes, one question lingers: if prying open the oyster is what's important, why do we parade around the expression of the world being our oyster?

The proverb originated in 1602 from Shakespeare's play *The Merry Wives of Windsor*.

"I will not lend thee a penny," a knight huffed at one of his followers.

His follower, an underdog in his own right, was unflinching. "Why, then, the world's mine oyster, Which I with sword will open."[59]

Whether it was for marketability or ease, the follower's dialogue was shortened over time to the mere idiom, "the world is your oyster."

And so, the world *is* your oyster. There are opportunities and ideas nested just about everywhere. The magic is in learning to pry the world open. You might not need a Shakespearean-era sword for it, but a few tricks up your sleeve wouldn't hurt.

FIND YOUR SAFETY NET

Akshay's environment allowed him to learn from his start-up failures and eventually find success. Still, his story may seem out of reach. Most people don't have the privilege of attending a university like Stanford, where pearls are abundant.

The thought lurked in my mind for many months after talking to Akshay. Was the *entire* world your oyster? Or did you have to get accepted into an environment already rich with pearls?

I explained my dilemma to Dr. Phillip Kim, a professor at Babson College who has studied entrepreneurship in various contexts across the Americas, Europe, and Asia. You can innovate in most environments, he told me, "but only if you optimize your environment for making mistakes."

Innovation is far from a linear process. As Akshay did, you have to fail many times to unlock the full benefits of your environment. And you cannot fail freely if your environment makes it costly to do so. You cannot pry open the oyster if you don't have the proper glove on—a safety net to protect against slicing your hand open.[60]

Dr. Kim explained that the value you get from an environment is not intrinsic to its inherent worth. Instead, it's a product of your ability to make mistakes there. "Let's say you have limited resources, and you go to Silicon Valley or New York," he said. "It'd be a great experience, but if your idea doesn't work out, you might have to leave because the living costs are so high."

If you cannot afford to make mistakes in an environment, you cannot reap its benefits of innovation.

What would make it safer for you to fail? The answer is different for everyone, so the features of the perfect environment are different for everyone too.

Akshay was an immigrant from India. He needed the ability to stay in the United States to make it safe for him to fail. The Bay Area was filled with large tech companies willing to sponsor immigrants. While he fumbled with start-ups, he also applied diligently for jobs at large companies. Microsoft eventually offered him a job, which gave him a safety net.

Your safety net could be something else. If entrepreneurship is looked down upon in your culture, it could be not telling your family when you start. If you struggle with mental health, it could be going for regular therapy sessions. The goal is to make it safer to endure the grueling process of prying open an oyster by optimizing your environment for innovation and new discoveries.

But what if you still cannot find those darn pearls?

PURSUE CHANGE

Russian author Leo Tolstoy famously said, "Everyone thinks of changing the world, but no one thinks of changing himself."[61]

Sometimes, though, changing your corner of the world is how you change yourself. Intentionally pursuing new environments is key to using your surroundings for innovation. When you stay in one place for a long time, you cozy up to the comfort of stagnancy. Familiarity rarely sparks growth.

The problem is that resistance to change is hardwired into our brains. "The more you do something, the more ingrained it becomes in neural pathways," clinical psychologist Dr. Sanam Hafeez describes. "It's like how a computer stores the sites you visit. When you log onto your browser, they will pop up because you use them a lot." Change disarrays all the information your brain has learned to adapt to the status quo.

Yet, this is exactly why change is important. "If you stretch your brain past its comfort zone, you're opening the door to being receptive to other types of change," Hafeez notes.[62] A fresh, new browser page can help spark a new idea. Changing your environment—whether it's transferring to a different school or moving from a city to the countryside—keeps your mind on its toes. When your mind is alert, you're more prone to innovation.

Akshay is a master at this. In less than thirty-five years, he grew up in India, went to Purdue University in Indiana for his undergraduate degree, attended Stanford in the Bay Area, worked at LinkedIn in India again, and then ended up back in the States as the COO at a rapidly growing start-up called Notion. When I asked him what his favorite part of working at Notion was, he said, "I like that we've switched offices three times already." There are new pearls to discover in every new place you go.

A simpler example is changing your workspace. When I change the café I write in, I experience a boost to my creative processes. I'm much more attuned to my environment and the opportunities it carries. I'm more likely to chat with the barista, note the atmosphere, and meet new people. It has led to some of my most thought-provoking conversations and creative ideas.

Other times, all it takes to spark creativity is working on the floor instead of at a desk.[63] Pearls come in all shapes and sizes.

* * *

One entrepreneur I spoke with while writing this book was particularly passionate about bringing change for refugees. When she was trying to figure out how she could help, she visited a Greek refugee camp located on an olive grove. There, she met women who had experienced some of the worst horrors in the world.

The women saw the olive grove as an opportunity to bond and create—they saw it as a pearl. They would make olive oil while telling her about the experiences that had brought them to the camp. Innovation is relative to your environment. Something as simple as olive oil can be a powerful sign of resilience when your future is otherwise uncertain.

There are pearls hiding in every corner of the world. There are new people to meet, unexpected skills to learn, and ideas waiting to be created. Thinking about your environment with intention means treating every place like an oyster. While prying it open looks a bit different everywhere, one day, the pearls will greet you in all their shimmer.

PRY OPEN THE OYSTER

- Environments offer you pearls. Innovation happens when you actively seek them out.

- Reflect on your current environment(s). What are its strengths? What is it known for? For each strength, note if it's something you utilize currently. If not, consider if and how you can.

- Write down all the ways you interact with your environment on a daily basis. Consider the elements of your environment you regularly leave out of your routine. Engaging with these elements can help spark new ideas and opportunities.

- Constancy fosters stagnation. Regularly change your environment, whether it be in a small or large way.

CHAPTER 4

BE YOUR OWN AIR PURIFIER

———

Don't get stuck in how the world exists today. Embrace the freedom of knowing that you can change it.

—LISA SEACAT DELUCA

Most days in the suburbs, you probably marvel at how plainly uninteresting the things around you are. But some days, you might just see a girl proudly clutching a plate to her head with a large shower curtain taped to it.

That's the suburbs for you.

The girl would be Lisa Seacat DeLuca. She was in second grade and had just made her first "invention," a solution to all the umbrellas in the world that can't keep your feet dry in the rain. The shower curtain extended to the ground, keeping her entirely dry. What Lisa didn't know at the time was that this first invention would be one of many. *Six hundred patents* many.

How did this little girl go from stumbling in shower curtains to being the most prolific inventor in IBM's history?

✳ ✳ ✳

In America, the Digital Revolution had taken root by the 1980s, with computers making their way onto desks across the country.[64] Many of the early computer scientists pioneering the revolution were women. A woman created an early prototype of the internet.[65] A woman created the first WHOIS directory. A woman wrote the documentation for the programming language used to create the Macintosh.[66]

In a time when most women were secretaries, teachers, and bookkeepers, computing was relatively untouched by the stereotypes that plagued the rest of society. Women raced to university to learn about the burgeoning field. In 1983, more than 36 percent of computer science majors were women.

But by 2014, that number had dropped to 18 percent. While the percentage of women in other professional jobs had risen sharply, computer science was a plummeting exception.[67] Experts were bewildered—what had gone wrong?

An inventor's journey may have some answers.

Lisa and I spoke at seven a.m.[68] When I greeted her with a groggy "good morning," she beamed at me.

"What was growing up in Montana like?" I asked her. It was a leading question: I knew the state had a reputation for not much happening at all.

Lisa seemed unbothered by my implication. Her eyes lit up as she explained to me that in places with more to do, "you're constantly rushing to the zoo or the aquarium." There's less to leave to the imagination. But in Montana, Lisa got to *make* things exciting. Her imagination could run through the long stretches of grasslands freely.

Where would her mind wander? One place was computers.

Personal computers were becoming increasingly mainstream during the 1980s. They were thought-provoking tools that gave you a new lens to see the world through. For the times when you weren't looking to have your thoughts provoked, they had games. With just one device, you could play arcade-style table tennis, shoot up some aliens, and guide PAC-MAN through the maze of his universe.

In a 1985 Apple advertisement, a young boy is shown running to catch his bus. "This morning, Brian Scott made a career decision," the narrator begins. "His first giant step? Learning to use an Apple."

The ad continues to spotlight the child at school where he uses an Apple computer to play various games, from outer space to biology-themed ones. "Whatever Brian wants to be, an Apple personal computer can help him be it."

There is a reason "Brian" was not "Brianna." His classmates are mostly boys. There is one girl (aside from the teacher) in the entire commercial, and Brian turns off her computer as she is working. She rolls her eyes.[69]

Apple was not the only company marketing computers to male customers. Games had always been seen as something for boys. When computers went from innovative technology to household staple toys, computers also went from "for everyone" to "for boys."[70]

With this shift, the stories of the past decades of women pioneering the field were lost. Today, when you look for important computer scientists on Google, a row of men pops up. It's the phenomenon of bro culture: the more the field was advertised for men, the more it became inhospitable to women.[71]

But talking to Lisa, it didn't seem like she was affected by the pervading culture in technology. "I loved video games, the thrill of pressing a button and watching the character suddenly respond," she told me. "I fell in love with computer science before I even knew what computer science was."

How was she able to fall in love with computers in such a stereotype-ridden world?

To answer this question, let's zoom out. So far, we've talked about environments in the context of optimizing and embracing them. When choosing environments, we look for frontiers, and when we're immersing ourselves in those environments, we seek pearls. But as you might know, if you've ever had a dust allergy, some parts of our environment are better off filtered away.

The trick is in learning to be your own air purifier.

As award-winning filmmaker David Lynch says, "Negativity is the enemy of creativity."[72] In order to unlock the innovative potential of your environment, you have to separate out the bad stuff first.

Lisa is amazing at purifying her environment.

When I asked her if the male-targeted messaging of video games ever discouraged her, she shrugged. "I didn't have a lot of friends, so my siblings were my friends. My brother never hesitated to play with me and he didn't treat me differently just because I was a girl."

Distancing herself from the stereotypes around her allowed Lisa to freely explore technology. After high school, she attended Carnegie Mellon University, one of the best schools in the world for computer science. Here, she began charting her path as an inventor.

* * *

While we're on the topic of universities, let's make a quick detour to my school, UC Berkeley. It's situated in California's sunny Bay Area right next to Silicon Valley, a place brimming with entrepreneurial opportunity. But as I've met fellow students, many are unhappy. In fact, Berkeley consistently ranks as having one of the most depressed and stressed-out student bodies in the country.

I remember walking around campus on my first day, dazed. In an environment with so much possibility, how were people not bursting at the seams with excitement?

It's because humans are naturally *horrible* at being their own air purifiers. "Students want to make the most of their time at Berkeley," one alumnus explained to me. "They want to be successful. And success means working at the top firms in the country."

With over thirty thousand students at the school and only a few precious spots open at the top companies, getting a job feels like a race to the top. By the time they graduate, people are too out of breath to enjoy the run or the prize.

The result is a lot of missed pearls.[73] "I ended up hating the job I spent four years trying to land," the alumnus admitted.

At the beginning of each school year, clubs line the university entrance with tables advertising their offerings. While the consulting tables are often packed with eager freshmen asking questions, the countless entrepreneurship tables are notably sparser. With so many people ultimately regretting their fixation on corporate success, why does the pattern continue year after year?

Esteemed polymath René Girard's mimetic theory might have some answers. Mimetic theory suggests people are imitators. We imitate each other's actions and desires, even if we don't fundamentally share those same desires.[74] Students mimetically fall trap to each other's desires for corporate success. In reality, only a few students feel a sense of satisfaction and belonging when they finally make it to the shiny company.

How can you let your environment energize you instead of rope you into conformity?

* * *

Straight out of college, Lisa found herself at IBM, a company known for encouraging invention among its employees.

In the early 2000s, it was far too easy to feel like a little fish in a big pond at IBM. The company was at the forefront of technology. With a long history of rapid innovation, Lisa had big shoes to fill, but as she looked at all the patents hanging above people's desks, she felt a thrill. She wanted one for herself.

She got to work.

She built a system that let you know if a cup of coffee in your car was empty. If it was, it directed you to the nearest coffee shop. She built a search engine powered by your voice. It detected the nuances in how you explained what you wanted in order to give you more accurate search results.

Over a decade later, she's acquired more than six hundred patents and is considered the most prolific inventor in IBM's more than century-long history. I imagine she must have fought many obstacles—from gender stereotypes to competition—to get to where she is today. When I asked her about them, she merely shrugged. She had purified her environment of them already.

Air purifiers take in all the air particles around them and selectively return the "good" particles back into the air. The magic is in the selection process of choosing what to output. There are two actions the purifier can take: sanitization and filtration. In other words, it can either output a cleansed version of the particle or get rid it entirely.

How can we figure out which parts of our environment to filter and which parts to sanitize?

SANITIZING

For all my Berkeley friends and any of you who feel plagued by competition, you don't have to call it quits just yet.

Competition, at its core, is rooted in a desire to grow, to get better, to be better. It can inspire you to work harder and maximize your potential. If you are someone motivated by competition, you can enjoy the benefits without being bogged down by toxicity.

The trick is in sanitization.

Sanitizing neutralizes. When you sanitize your environment, you change something about your environment in order to neutralize a bad effect. When you're stuck in an environment that isn't wholly toxic, sanitizing is key to being your own air purifier.

Pinpoint what you need to feel mentally well. Is it a healthy distance between work and free time? Schedule time every week to do things you enjoy outside of your job. Stick to it like you stick to your work calls. Is it merely less competition? Prioritize high performance in just one aspect of your environment. Aim for good grades in only one of your classes each semester.

You can choose to be inspired by competition without letting it control how you make all of your decisions.

Another toxin that has become overwhelmingly common in the twenty-first century is a lack of work-life balance. According to a study published by the *American Sociological Review*, a lack of work-life balance is leading to 70 percent of Americans feeling "stressed, overwhelmed, and maxed out."[75] As a solution, the study proposed reducing how much you work—whether it's working fewer shifts, taking more vacation days, or working fewer hours a day.

For Lisa, the solution was remote work. She's been working remotely since 2005, her second year at IBM. "I love it," she told me. "As a working mother, there are so many advantages to being with your kids. When I go into an office, I feel like I don't get as much done." She leans into the IBM inventing community remotely, without feeling overwhelmed by the omnipresence of work in physical offices.

Remote work allowed Lisa to sanitize her environment of the pressure many employees feel to overwork. It's also helped her stay innovative. Most of Lisa's more than six hundred patents have been made from the comfort of her cozy Montana home. In 2015, *Fast Company* ranked her as one of the most creative people in the world. She was named one of LinkedIn's Top 10 Next Wave of Enterprise Technologists Under 35. In 2019, *Innovation & Tech Magazine* declared her their Innovator of the Year.

The goal of sanitizing is to modify your environment while still enjoying its other benefits. But what happens if you can't find a way to modify it? How do you know your environment is worth sanitizing?

FILTERING

It was 2005 and Stewart Butterfield felt unimportant.

He was working at Yahoo! after his company, Flickr, had been acquired by the tech giant. "It was so hard to get the resources that [the Flickr team] needed," he reflected later. "I think we missed out on so many opportunities where Flickr could have been a lot bigger and more successful than it was as part of Yahoo!—because of Yahoo!'s internal 'screwed up-ness.'"[76] With all of its corporate bureaucracy, Yahoo! made it impossible for Stewart to build out the dream he had for his product.

Every air purifier encounters red flag toxins it just gets rid of—whether it be dust or constant bickering with a manager.

No amount of work-life balance can neutralize the effects of feeling devalued. Hearing Butterfield's story, most people would probably agree he should leave Yahoo! and pursue a career on his own terms.

But while spotting toxins seems fairly obvious when we're judging other people's lives, the difference is subtler when we reflect inward. This is our bias blind spot: while we can see how bias is hindering other people's judgments, we do not see the same role of bias in our decisions.[77] We shrug and tell Butterfield to just leave Yahoo!, but hesitate to leave our own toxic work environment.

Bias blind spots are rampant at Berkeley. Seeking prestige is so normalized among students that we don't realize it creates an environment of never feeling good enough.

So, what's the solution?

If you can't find a way to sanitize your environment or are unsure if it's even worth it to try, do the Toxin Test by asking yourself these two questions:

1. Does your environment make you want to keep your head down? This is the feeling of not wanting to stand out, in fear of some consequence, like being socially ostracized or losing your job.

2. Does your environment kill your motivation or opportunities for success? Either your dreams *seem* impossible or the toxin directly *makes* your dreams impossible.

If your answer to either of these questions is "yes," your environment has passed the Toxin Test. You're dealing with a red flag toxin too pesky to be sanitized—it needs to be filtered.

To effectively filter out such toxins, you need to spend time actively reflecting on the environments you interact with. Put each one through the Toxin Test. If an environment passes, it cannot be salvaged. Your efforts cannot detoxify it.

In other words, it's time to start packing your bags.[78]

Butterfield quit Yahoo! to start another company. In 2020, that company, Slack, was bought by Salesforce for $27.7 billion.[79] To say his filtration was effective is an understatement. He is one of the most successful entrepreneurs of his time.

One of my Berkeley friends recently dropped her second major to explore some of the "less practically applicable" courses in college. It's a way for her to discover the things she loves while ridding herself of the toxic environment she experienced in her second major.

Just like in air purifiers, real-life filtration comes in all shapes and sizes.

HOW TO PURIFY YOUR ENVIRONMENT

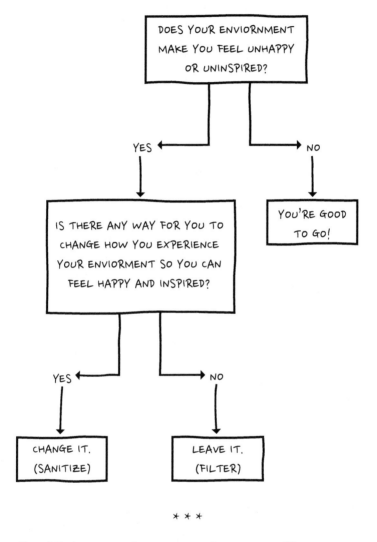

* * *

Shetal Shah is a son of immigrants who grew up selling newspapers and tending to his neighbors' lawns. He started his career on Wall Street as an investment banker, but quickly realized corporate hierarchies weren't for him. He wanted something to call his own. So, he decided to try out entrepreneurship.

It started with opening a franchisee with Dunkin Donuts. Securing a $1 million loan from the US Small Business Administration, he worked to get his store up and running. Some nights, he was sleeping on 150-pound donut bags.

But just as his efforts began paying off, Dunkin Donuts headquarters changed its financing model. Though the corporate team had been the ones to encourage Shah to pursue the SBA loan, they now saw it as a liability. They began to put pressure on him to accelerate repayment. They went from seeing him as their "emerging star" to a "high risk asset."

Shah knew a red flag toxin when he saw one, so he set out to build something better on his own.

He opened Frappe Joe Coffee, a place where Mediterranean flavors and old-world spices were infused with traditional coffee shop food and drinks. In an industry dominated by European flavors, Shah's tiny shop succeeded on creativity. In fact, much of this book was fueled by his cardamom-rose lattes and bagels with *baba ghanoush*. Innovation can be the secret to large corporate success, but it can also be the secret to your local coffee shop's magic. All it takes is one person being bold enough to be his own air purifier.

Now, let's take a step back.

For air purifiers to be effective, they need to be able to take in all the particles around them. Only then can they process the particles thoughtfully, either through filtering or sanitizing. Before applying all the nuances and complexities and fun metaphors that have filled this section on Intentional

Environment, we have to know what's around us. Intentionality starts with awareness.

In order to decide what to do with our environment or what kinds of environments we want to seek, we have to first process where we are right now thoroughly and with an open mind. We need to think about how we react to our environment and *why*.

Then, we can get creative with the metaphors—air purifiers, oysters, and all.

BE YOUR OWN AIR PURIFIER

- We encounter various environments every day. As you go about your life the next few days, take note of each one. How do you intuitively react to them? How do you feel when you step into a new one? How do you feel when you leave?

- If your environment makes you feel scared, anxious, or otherwise upset, think about why. Can you neutralize the negative effect it has on you? Consider the personal boundary that environment breaks and if you can reinstate it.

- Put every environment you experience through the Toxin Test. Does your environment make you want to keep your head down? Does your environment kill your motivation or opportunities for success? If the answer to either of these questions is yes, create a plan of the steps you can take to leave your environment.

PART II

INTENTIONAL

CONVERSATION

CHAPTER 5

CURIOSITY NEVER KILLED THE UNDERDOG

———

We're all human. We all have questions. Let's just ask them and own them and have some fun while we're doing it.

—KINSEY GRANT

When I was little, my grandpa fondly used to call me *khakhoran*, ruffling my hair with his playfully cocked eyebrows and a grin. The rough translation from Hindi would be "constant questioner."

He was the kind of person who collected facts and historical dates for fun. He loved answering questions as much as I loved asking them. But I thought of him as a rare exception to the adult world. Most adults, I quickly discovered, hated questions. Everyone from my schoolteacher to my fourth cousin's neighbor's aunt rolled their eyes when I asked "why?" Eventually, I stopped asking.

It's a normal occurrence for kids around the world. Three-year-old children ask an average of twenty-seven questions an hour, but as those children go to elementary school, the number drops to *three* questions an hour. By the time they're ten, the average number is virtually zero.[80]

Still, the most curious children tend to perform the best in math and reading.[81] It makes sense: curious children care most about genuinely understanding what they're learning. This translates to better academic performance.

For socioeconomically disadvantaged children, the association between curiosity and academic achievement is much stronger. Many child psychologists even cite curiosity as an overlooked solution to bridging achievement gaps across socioeconomic classes.[82] While your grandma may lament the deaths of all the cats curiosity killed, one fact is clear: curiosity has never killed an underdog.

How can underdogs use curiosity to guide their innovation?

* * *

Fast-forwarding a couple of years after my love for questions faded, I discovered a daily email newsletter that sent a digest of all the business news for the day. It was written in as fun a tone as you can make stocks and insurance by a small media company called Morning Brew.

In October of 2020, Morning Brew was acquired by *Business Insider* for 75 million dollars.[83] In an era where marketers lament that email is dead, this is a company making millions from the medium. More importantly, its target market is the exact demographic experts say email is dead for: Gen Z and Millennials.

With so many disadvantages, how has the company managed to thrive in the media industry?

When founder Alex Lieberman was in college, he would help his friends prepare for job interviews. Each time he asked them how they stayed up to date with business news, he noticed they all had the "same canned answer"—they claimed they read *The Wall Street Journal,* but very few actually read it cover-to-cover. It was too dense.

In response, Lieberman created a newsletter to help his intellectually curious friends keep up with current events in an easy-to-digest form. His friend, Austin Rief, joined as a cofounder soon after and the two never looked back. What started as a PDF file emailed out to peers is now a multi-million-dollar company.[84]

Lieberman and Rief are in their twenties and ever curious. One of their first employees, Kinsey Grant, described it as part of the team's competitive advantage. "They're willing to ask questions about the things they don't know," she told me. "That helps them find the answers to get ahead."

Having questions doesn't seem like too tough of a feat. From an evolutionary standpoint, curiosity is necessary for an animal's survival. The bird that eats its lifetime of berries from the same old bush may never discover the more nutritious bush around the corner.[85] The world rewards exploration, so natural selection chose curiosity. Now, humans are hardwired to ask questions.

How can we all embrace the confidence to ask them?

✶ ✶ ✶

Peter Thiel is one of the most famous business thinkers in the world. He cofounded billion-dollar companies PayPal and Palantir Technologies. He was Facebook's first external investor. He was one of the earliest funders of Yelp and LinkedIn.[86]

One of Thiel's closest business partners, Michael Gibson, describes walking into a conference room one day where Thiel was sitting with seven scholars. All the room's occupants were staring intently at the same book.

"What are they doing?" Gibson asked Thiel's assistant, bewildered.

"Reading chapter seven of *The City and Man* by Leo Strauss," she told him.

The eight thinkers stayed in the same room for eight hours that day. It was all for one chapter on ancient philosophy.[87]

The thing about curiosity is that we worry too much about if it is productive. We hesitate to spend our day poring over ideas we're curious about because we don't want it to be a waste of our time. But taking our curiosity seriously, as Thiel did, is key to innovation.

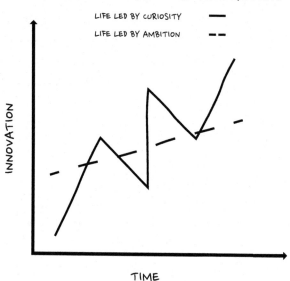

YOUR POTENTIAL FOR INNOVATION

LIFE LED BY CURIOSITY ——

LIFE LED BY AMBITION – –

INNOVATION

TIME

Kinsey is also someone who takes her curiosity *very* seriously.

I discovered her through Morning Brew's podcast, *Business Casual*. Each episode began with the sound of coffee pouring and then an energetic voice: "Hey there and welcome to *Business Casual*, the podcast from Morning Brew answering the biggest questions in business. I'm your host and Brew business editor, Kinsey Grant. And now, let's get into it!"

She was not kidding. She really did get *into* it, tackling the biggest questions in business with some of the biggest people in it.

When billionaire entrepreneur and television personality Mark Cuban told her about how he paid his employees despite the coronavirus pandemic, she was quick to ask if people with limited resources could really do the same: "How do you go about making that decision if you are running a chain of five coffee shops in rural Florida?"[88] And when *HuffPost* founder Arianna Huffington discussed the issue of burnout among business executives, Kinsey had to know why it even mattered when they were already making billions: "Is there any sort of tangible fallout from all of this?"[89]

Business Casual made it easy to forget Kinsey was just twenty-five. She asked the questions no one was ready to voice to the people with some of the most power in our economy.

Her curiosity was not in vain. In Investopedia's list of 2020's "Top 10 Business Podcasts," *Business Casual* ranked fourth. It was also the only podcast on the list hosted by someone under the age of thirty. Within a year of launching the podcast, it hit 1 million downloads.

Kinsey's success is rooted in her curiosity. Her willingness to ask questions and her drive to see them answered opens opportunities most twenty-five-year-olds don't dare to dream of.

Kinsey was the first person I interviewed for this book. Before our talk, I practiced the questions I had prepared for her out loud in the mirror until even my reflection had them memorized. Still, when it came time for our call, my heart was beating rapidly.

"How do you get the courage to challenge some of the most influential figures in business?" I asked. At the time, I wasn't looking for book content. I just needed some advice to get through the interview.

She shrugged. "We're all human. We all have questions. Let's just ask them and own them and have some fun while we're doing it."

Her words slowed my heart rate down enough to survive the call. But back in the real world, owning our curiosity is easier said than done. You need to love information enough to want to seek it.

It's a love especially crucial for underdogs. Kinsey is white, conventionally attractive, and employed—privileges she openly acknowledges. Still, as a young woman, her credibility in the media industry is often undermined.

People have told her she shouldn't host a podcast because of the sound of her voice. They have asked her pityingly, "Are you in the right place, sweetie?" when she certainly was. When Jordan Belfort, the former stockbroker known as "The Wolf of Wall Street" found out Kinsey was the same age as his daughter, he stopped answering her interview questions seriously.

Through all this, curiosity is what gives Kinsey fire. That passion for information is in her DNA. She grew up doing crossword puzzles with her dad on Sunday mornings. It encouraged her to stay well-informed on what was happening in the world. In fifth grade, she did her first news story ever at school on Pajama Day. Standing in her polka-dot PJs, she realized she loved giving people the information they needed. This kind of love for information naturally lends itself to inquisitiveness.

But how does inquisitiveness lend itself to innovation?

* * *

In 2021, Kinsey left Morning Brew. "What happened?" I asked her. The people were great at Morning Brew. She loved the podcast she was working on. The company was rapidly growing.

And yet, Kinsey felt a tug. She had done many episodes of *Business Casual* with content creators and entrepreneurs. "I wanted to know what it was all like," she said. Kinsey had talked about them. Now, she wanted to experience their life.

Her *Business Casual* partner Josh Kaplan had left the company a few months before. He had an email list with an assortment of people he had met in his life, from coworkers to college friends. He would send everyone a question like "should college athletes get paid?" People would hit Reply All with their answers. Josh called the list "Thinking is Cool."

"The conversations were pretty intense," Kinsey said. "They were awesome." For Josh, it was a way to bring together disparate groups of people in his life and start conversations. For

Kinsey, it was a flourishing online community way ahead of its time.[90]

In May of 2021, the two founded Thinking Is Cool, a media start-up inspired by its namesake and dedicated to making your next conversation better than your last. Like all of Kinsey's ventures, it started with a question (or four): "What if we all stopped to think a little harder? To have conversations without getting combative? To be honest and give ourselves time and space for nuance? What might the world look like?" These are questions Kinsey plans to spend the next couple of years figuring out.

The company releases podcast episodes weekly. In a landscape where the most popular podcasts feature rehashed interviews with the same celebrities, Thinking Is Cool talks about topics both diverse and divisive—everything from whether the "girl-boss" conforms to systems of oppression to whether late-stage capitalism is inherently unethical.

"I want to create a space where people can come together and share their ideas and feel safe about it," she told me. "I want to ask people hard questions. I want to talk to my friends about it. And I want to show people how they can do the same."

Fostering the kind of curiosity Kinsey has can seem difficult. When I was talking to her, I remember thinking, "Well, I could never have so many questions in the first place." I forgot about the little girl whose nickname was *khakhoran*.

Growing up in a world that discourages curiosity has caused us to filter out our questions in fear of appearing unintelligent. But it's not gone forever. How can we rekindle that childlike curiosity?

LET CURIOSITY LEAD YOU

It's hard to question everything. It's even harder to question things you don't find interesting.

Call up the question that randomly pops up in your mind sometimes. Think back to the last time an idea made you want to raise your eyebrows and tilt your head. Letting curiosity lead you means finding answers and learning about these things. Don't keep your mind on a leash—give it the freedom to wander where it wants to go.

One of the biggest misconceptions about curiosity is that it rivals efficiency. It's a false dichotomy—we assume we can only have one or the other, but curiosity can foster efficiency. As individuals, we are predisposed to liking the things we're better at doing.[91] Questions are an indicator of interest. When we chase the opportunities that tug at our curiosity, we are led on a path of things we are the best at.

Kinsey's tug is what led her to pursue journalism in the first place. Her high school headmaster had warned her mother: "There's no money in journalism. She's never going to get the job she wants." Still, Kinsey refused to deny her curiosity.

When she got to college, she was set on pursuing political journalism. Her family came from politics, and she'd grown up thinking it was her calling. When she got to college and took actual politics classes, she realized it wasn't for her.

Instead of worrying about what people would think if she switched paths, she took various classes she found interesting. Eventually, she settled on business journalism as a career. This would bring her to her success at Morning Brew.

For Kinsey, her path from letting curiosity lead her to creating something of her own was relatively short. But for most innovators, letting curiosity lead you has no immediate reward.

After dropping out of Reed College, Steve Jobs lingered around campus, admiring the posters throughout the halls—they were all hand-calligraphed. He just had to learn to do it himself.

Jobs decided to audit a calligraphy class at Reed. "It was beautiful, historical, artistically subtle in a way that science can't capture," he described with awe. At the same time, "none of this had even a hope of any practical application in my life."[92]

Ten years later, when he was designing Apple's first Macintosh computer, his knowledge of calligraphy came back to him, and he used it to design the computer's typeface. Today, Apple's typeface is key to its sleek design, one of its core competitive advantages.[93] Ironically, curiosity for the sake of curiosity reaps the highest reward in the end.

Being intentional with pursuing your curiosities creates room for new ideas and more questions, ultimately allowing you to see gaps for innovation you can fill. Because you're innovating off things that genuinely interest you, these explorations are more likely to be successful.

The benefits of letting curiosity lead you can take years to manifest. How do you keep yourself motivated to stay on a path that feels fruitless?

SEEK HIGH-REWARD CURIOSITY

Let's say you hear someone say the word "skeuomorph," a strange word you've never heard before. Immediately, the parts of your brain most sensitive to unpleasant sensations are on guard. They feel your uncertainty and they're not thrilled about it. Your brain then primes itself for answers by alerting the regions responsible for memory and learning.[94]

A skeuomorph is an object that imitates the design of a previous or similar iteration of itself. Your iPhone camera making a shuttering noise every time you click a picture is skeuomorphic. It's a sound reminiscent of the handheld cameras that came before them.

When you discover this fact, your brain retains the definition with heightened memory and sends dopamine messages to your body.[95]

One study by Harvard data scientist Tommy Blanchard investigated the orbitofrontal cortex, a part of your brain that helps you make decisions based on perceived reward value (i.e., figuring out whether to eat brussels sprouts or a brownie when you open the fridge).

What are people willing to do for a bit of relief from their questions? A lot, Blanchard discovered.

His study found many primates willing to give up basic human needs, like a sip of water, in exchange for satisfying their curiosity.[96] Curiosity has a very tangible reward in your brain. It might even be the reason you're dehydrated all the time.

The problem is this process has been somewhat reversed by societal norms. There's a common misconception that in order to be high-functioning, you need to have all the answers. It's been instilled into our brains since our first elementary school teacher chided, "Don't ask me dumb questions."

Over time, this has programmed people to treat questions as a sign of stupidity.[97] The famous French philosopher, Blaise Pascal, even described curiosity as mere vanity.[98] How can we reclaim our curiosity?

There are two types of curiosity, according to psychologist Jordan Litman: D-curiosity and I-curiosity. D-curiosity comes from "deprivation." This is the kind of curiosity you are likely most familiar with. It's the feeling of discomfort you experience when you don't know something, like the definition of a skeuomorph. When D-curiosity is satisfied, the reward is comfort. Think back to the last time you sat through a conversation and didn't know what everyone else was talking about. Remember how you felt when someone *finally* filled you in? That was your D-curiosity being fulfilled.

On the other hand, I-curiosity comes from "interest." This is the kind of curiosity you feel when you're generally interested in learning more about a topic. There's no deficit to fill because your goal isn't to find something specific. It's just to learn for the sake of knowing more.[99] It's the way you feel when you go down the Google rabbit hole of reading obscure articles about the history of ice cream trucks (trust me, I've been there).[100]

To reclaim and foster your curiosity, you need to maximize the dopamine you get out of curiosity. You'll find that high reward in I-curiosity. When you seek information without a specific end goal in mind, the dopamine released is higher. When your desire for knowledge is rewarded, you seek it more often, creating a positive feedback loop of curiosity. On the quest to become more curious, I-curiosity is your best friend.

✳ ✳ ✳

My mother is a preschool teacher, but in college, she studied business. As years of working at a nearby school passed, one question was always on her mind: *what would it be like to have something I can call my own?*

One day, she quit her job.

In our sunroom that connects the rest of our house to the backyard, she placed an easel, wooden shelves filled with activities, and a rug. The next day, she taught a child there. Just a few months later, she registered our bustling sunroom as a business with the New Jersey government as "Neev Montessori." School was officially in session.

Now, she glows. Her days revolve around her students. She teaches them everything from tidying up to reading their first book. "I don't know how she does it," their parents tell me, shaking their heads. "But I am so grateful she does." My mother let curiosity lead her, and many people now benefit from her creativity.

We live in an era where asking questions has never been harder. As we seek efficiency, we often sacrifice curiosity in the process. For some, exploration threatens the stability of the status quo with the unknown. For others, curiosity represents vanity; for many, curiosity is intimidating because it leaves us feeling dumb and vulnerable.

Asking questions is crucial dialogue when you're looking to turn your disadvantages around through innovation. To chart uncharted paths, you have to explore ideas unfamiliar to you.

It's an exploration easier for the underdog. We don't have all the answers and the status quo is often uncomfortable for us. That gives us all the fire we need to be curious.

So, seek truth. Ask questions—the more uncomfortable the better. The best case? Mark Cuban sitting across from you in a couple of years. The worst? Your mom rolling her eyes.

If you get called a *khakhoran* in the process, you'll know you're doing something right.

CURIOSITY NEVER KILLED THE UNDERDOG

- Write down questions as soon as they pop into your mind. When you feel those butterflies of excitement, it's a sign you've stumbled upon something worth exploring.

- Let curiosity lead you through your life path instead of societal norms around money and prestige. You will thrive in spaces that naturally pique your interest.

- Foster your I-curiosity, or the curiosity that comes from interest. Instead of treating curiosity as a tool to fill gaps in your knowledge, use it to learn more about things in general.

CHAPTER 6

THROW THE DINNER PARTY

How do you get a seat at the dinner table? Plan the party.

—ANGELA LUNA

There were two kinds of kids in elementary school: the ones who did what was cool and the ones who decided what was cool.

"Cool" came in two flavors: mainstream and counterculture. Some people got their high off being popular. Others got it from not fitting into what was considered popular.

I was the counterculture kid who did what was cool. I had a Pinterest board of emo fashion I scrolled through for inspiration. I wore my bootcut jeans proudly with T-shirts of bands I had never heard of. Being called "normal" was the worst kind of insult to me.

Social structures from elementary school transfer over into the real world, with a few dashes of extra nuance. A lot of entrepreneurship happens among the kids who decide what is counterculture cool. In actively defying the status quo, they innovate. After all, who is Elon Musk but a CEO who doesn't want to be like *other* billionaires?

Angela Luna was an Elon Musk at her high school. I got to sit down with her for a talk and I had to know: how can we all be counterculture leaders too?

✶ ✶ ✶

It was September of 2015. Angela was a student at Parsons School of Design. Her goal was the same as almost everyone else in her class: spend life creating luxurious clothes for wealthy New Yorkers. On this particular day, Angela was scrolling idly through Facebook. One picture made her stop in her tracks.

She was staring at three-year-old Alan Kurdi, a Syrian refugee whose lifeless body lay on the sands of a Turkish beach. He and his family had been on a boat to a new life in Canada when it had capsized.

Alan was one of over 3,770 refugees who died crossing the Mediterranean that year.[101] The number 3,770 is likely a severe underestimate—most refugee deaths go unreported and unnoticed. Angela could feel her fists clench as she read more and more about the refugee crisis. "I never actually looked outside of social media to investigate what's going on in the world," she admitted. "It's embarrassing to say, but this finally broke me outside my bubble."

While Angela was ready to leave her current life behind and pursue a career as a humanitarian, her mother had other plans for her. "I paid for you to go to design school," she huffed, "so you're getting your degree from Parsons."

It felt like Angela's mother had crushed her life calling before Angela could even pull up the International Rescue Committee's website. Her options seemed limited: she could become the couture designer she'd planned to be or defy her mother and become a humanitarian.

Angela went to one of her professors with her dilemma, hoping for a third option. Was there any way she could use fashion to raise awareness for the refugee crisis?

Her professor shook her head, scoffing, "It's not possible." Fashion was designed to embody a fantasy world—tying it to something so horrific and real would defeat the purpose. "Let fashion be what it is."

A life of couture was looming near the horizon. What could possibly be her way out?

* * *

Angela grew up in an all-girls Catholic school. She was the kind of kid I would have looked up to in elementary school. She probably grinned with pride when someone found her weird—it would mean she'd successfully pushed back on their beliefs.

She used to design feminine gowns draped in elegant toilet paper to prance around in at home but wore masculine suits to school to protest gender norms. Her goal was always to challenge the status quo and create dialogue. She didn't care what people whispered about her in the process.

When Angela was in fifth grade, all the girls in her class would sit at the same lunch table. The conversations were similar every day. She never felt like she truly belonged.

One day, she got tired of being the outsider. So, she plopped herself down at an entirely different table. She was by herself, but she was no longer an outsider. It was *her* table.

She spent three whole days shifting around on the cafeteria bench by herself. But after a while, some of the girls moved to sit with her. Because it was her table, Angela could talk about the things she liked with them. When the conversation grew boring again, she merely started a new table again. She would sit alone for a few days, but she wasn't concerned. She knew the right people would find her eventually. Angela didn't just participate in lunchtime conversations—she *started* them.

When you're the underdog, it's tempting to try and fit into the status quo conversation. But in the status quo, you will always remain the underdog. Activist, philosopher, and feminist Grace Lee Boggs says "we are the leaders we've been waiting for."[102] To lead successfully, we have to create the conversation we've been waiting for.

The question that remains: how?

* * *

Louis XIV became the most powerful person in France at the ripe age of five years old.[103] Growing up into so much power, it seemed inevitable he would fall into vanity. He created a lavish dress code for his court and wore colorful, billowing clothes that draped around his body. He dressed to intimidate his rivals and impress his people. Being wealthy in his land meant being able to afford to wear whatever trends he found impressive. The French nobles went broke trying to keep up.[104]

Seventeenth-century France is a microcosm of the modern luxury fashion world: it is a performance.

Luxury fashion was never meant to be utilitarian. It is a tool to set the wealthy apart from the poor. The culture of the wealthy who wear luxury has always been philanthropic—they give spare cash to the underprivileged rather than try to serve their actual needs.

In order to *make* a difference in the refugee crisis, Angela had to *be* different from the current conversations in couture.

So, she decided to channel that same energy of her fifth-grade self unabashedly flouncing over to an empty table. She decided to start a new conversation in the fashion industry: a collection of clothes that served the needs of refugees.

She created burnt orange trench coats that turned into tents with the pull of a string. She created olive green backpacks that zipped up into capes. Most importantly, she created reflective coats that doubled as inflatable life jackets, so refugees traveling on boats would have a lifeline if their boat capsized. The pieces were beautiful, yet distinctly utilitarian.

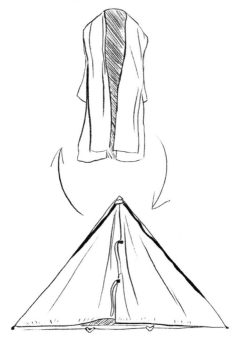

The trench coat Angela designed turns into a tent.

Angela's collection won the Parsons Designer of the Year award. Soon, people around the city began murmuring about the possibilities of socially conscious fashion.

Why did it work?

* * *

A mentor of mine once told me about her passion for diversity in entrepreneurship. She was frustrated with the lack of inclusivity in the space and wanted to participate in dialogue around these issues. The problem? She wasn't an entrepreneur. She was an executive at a rapidly growing start-up, but that never felt like enough to her.

We often shy away from spaces we feel underqualified to be in. As my computer science professor would tell me, if there is a barrier that seems insurmountable, it can probably just be short-circuited.

In programming and in life, certain things are technically impossible. For example, we cannot divide a number by zero—it will cause our code to crash. But let's say we are writing code for a couture designer. He wants to know how much money he has spent for every dress he sold. If he sold zero dresses on a particular day, the code we meticulously write for him will fail.

So we short-circuit.

```
number_of_dresses = 0 or total_money_spent/number_of_dresses
```

We tell our program that either the number of dresses will be zero *or* it should output the total money our designer spent divided by the number of dresses he sold. If the first statement is true, the program will skip over the second statement entirely. It will never get the chance to crash. Crisis averted.[105]

In the same way, you can either start a conversation *or* wait to be invited to a conversation. When you choose to start the conversation, you skip over needing an invitation to the status quo. You short-circuit being the underdog.

Can that short-circuiting lead to innovation?

* * *

Encouraged by the buzz around her collection, Angela began her own company fresh out of college. She called it ADIFF, after make "*a diff*erence."

As a twenty-two-year-old woman, she still had plenty of hurdles to cross. While in fashion, people were becoming receptive to the idea of humanitarian clothing, the venture capital scene was a different story. She struggled to secure funding, with investor after investor telling her she was too young or too early. Sometimes, they overlooked her entirely to speak to her male COO.

When investors proved they weren't ready to budge, Angela took her case to crowdfunding. Fashion start-ups were very rare in the crowdfunding scene, so she had the freedom to start a new dialogue with ADIFF.

Her campaign was featured by *Business Insider* and brought in $100,000. It was just enough for her to get started.

Because she's not at the mercy of any investors, Angela has been able to keep ADIFF and its goals fluid. As she grows ADIFF, she's discovered many issues within the fashion industry and is working to tackle them. Her factories hire refugee employees and pay them a living wage. For every clothing item bought through ADIFF's website, one piece is donated to a refugee. ADIFF's clothes are made with traditionally unwanted or unusable materials.

Had she decided to use her work to simply raise money for the refugee crisis, Angela would have spent her twenties sitting in on conversations with other brands. But as the one pioneering the movement toward accessible, sustainable fashion with her work at ADIFF, Angela gets to throw the dinner parties in the industry. Big brands, who would have otherwise never spared a twenty-something-year-old woman a second glance, want to sit at her lunch table. It doesn't hurt that she was invited to the same fashion awards show as Beyoncé. It's a cool place to be.

How can you throw your own glamorous dinner party?

YOU DON'T NEED A MANSION

If you're reading this and thinking you don't have any novel ideas to throw dinner parties for, I was thinking the same thing after I finished my talk with Angela. She was incredibly inspiring, but it felt like I couldn't achieve the same things she did.

There is limitless potential in our everyday spaces to challenge the norms of the status quo dialogue. Not every dinner party needs a lavish spread and mansion backdrop—they just need good conversation.

Let's take Alex Wieckowski. I got to sit down with Alex and talk to him soon after my chat with Angela. At first glance, he seems pretty ordinary. He grew up in New York and graduated from college a few years ago. Now, he has a nine-to-five job at a podcast company as a content writer.

The last time he ever went mountain biking, Alex was exhausted—exhausted enough that he completely missed the ditch straight in front of him. He went rolling down the ditch and ended up with a separated shoulder. He couldn't tie his own shoes for months. As a self-declared jock, he loved sports and missed playing basketball. For a while, it felt like he'd lost his sense of purpose.

One hobby Alex rekindled during this time was his love for books. Sitting in bed, he was able to devour information about the world, but he didn't feel like he had a place in the conversations around books. "I didn't feel 'academic' enough," he admitted to me.

Alex had nowhere else to go. So, he created his own little corner of the internet. It was a space for him to talk about all things books. He called it Alex & Books.

As the one starting the dialogue, he got to talk about books like any nerdy jock would. His list of favorite books from 2019 included both Tucker Max and Geoffrey Miller's book on dating, *What Women Want,* and Yuval Noah Harari's dense historical read, *Sapiens.*

Today, Alex has his own newsletter, podcast, Instagram, and an ordinary day job. His audience spans over one hundred thousand people. He regularly gets emails from people around the world thanking him. "I used to hate reading," one says. "You really inspired me to pick up books and start reading again." He's building bridges but, at the same time, he's living a completely ordinary life.

Dinner parties don't need mansions. Some just need a good bookshelf.

FIND YOUR LINGO

What comes to mind when you think of the color red?

For most people, it's likely something related to the word "stop." This is our associative memory at play. Though there is nothing inherent to the color red that would make us think we should stop, we have seen the two concepts side by side so many times that our neurons have linked them together in our brain.[106]

The idea of associative memory makes sense—we are constantly recognizing relationships. When we see our bed, we yawn. When we see our desk, we sit up slightly straighter.

Associative memory dictates how we speak, too. We use similar words to communicate different intents. Would you rather have a friend who is *different* or a friend who is *unique*? Most people would answer "unique" because of our positive association with the word.

When Angela was building out her fashion collection for her senior thesis, she was confronted with a lot of raised eyebrows. Professors fawned over her classmates' work while shrugging indifferently at hers. One professor ignored her work completely.

While the refugee organizations she spoke with were excited about her collection, the people in the fashion industry couldn't understand its value. Angela felt stuck.

The problem lay in her approach. Her classmates were explaining what their collections were inspired by, so Angela did the same. She told people her collection was "inspired by" the refugee crisis, but inspired was too tepid a word—her collection was more radical than that. To throw a dinner party, you need new conversation. As Angela later explained to me, new conversation requires "an entirely new dictionary."

She began to present her work differently. She said her collection "took influence" from displaced peoples, and it was designed to "directly address" the refugee crisis. It was a subtle change, but it was enough to alert people's brains: they could not rely on their preexisting associative memory when observing her work. In order to understand it, they needed to create a new association with new diction in their brains. Angela's clothes weren't made to bring awareness to the refugee crisis—they were made to begin solving it.

Buzz and conversation sparked at Parsons about the girl with the radically different senior thesis project. Whether they loved it or hated it, everyone thought it was something worth talking about. To entice people to your dinner party, you need your own lingo.

* * *

Growing up, I used video-streaming platform Vimeo for the times when other websites were too quick at detecting copyright infringements. Whether I wanted movie clips or entire seasons of TV shows, I used Vimeo like a bootleg YouTube.

Ten years later, YouTube was the second most visited website in the world. Vimeo was a $6 billion company that stands on its own in the digital video space.[107]

At the time of writing this book, Vimeo is led by CEO Anjali Sud, who stepped into the role back in 2017 when the platform still screamed "bootleg YouTube." Sud knew why people like me used Vimeo, and she knew it could not be the foundation for a billion-dollar company. The market was already saturated with companies doing what Vimeo was, but better. How could Sud innovate?

All the video platforms were playing the same game at the time. They made money from companies buying advertisements, so their goal was to attract as many viewers as possible.

In their obsession with viewers, creators were left in the dust.

Sud decided to bring a new business model to the space: SaaS (Software as a Service). Instead of being another platform for creators to put their videos, what if Vimeo made software for creators to craft better videos?

Sud reinvented the company to do just that. For all the mom and pop shops struggling to stay relevant in the age of Instagram, she created a video studio with templates. For the home instructors trying to earn a living, she created a video portal where they could livestream classes and put up paywalls wherever they wanted. For Fortune 500 companies who wanted to connect with their employees scattered around the world, she created a tool for them to have secure, internal video events.

Sud embraced radical change for a company that had been stagnant for years. By swerving its business model to focus on creators, she took Vimeo from participating in industrywide conversations to throwing the dinner party.[108]

In 2021, four years after she had first begun turning the company around, Sud took Vimeo public. By that time, 60 percent of the Fortune 500 had created an active account with Vimeo.[109] The industry was abuzz with dialogue on how to better support creators. Sud had successfully revived a once-forgotten brand and brought its power to an entirely new audience.

Twelve-year-old me could have never seen it coming.

As an underdog, you may not fit in with the chatter around you, but that means you have the freedom to create your own conversations. When you're the one initiating dialogue, you're the one in control. Don't try to be better than the people around you—be radically different. Speak with authority and people will lean in. You cannot be unqualified in a space you create.

There are many ways to throw a dinner party. Bring dialogue that's familiar to a new space like Alex did. Bring dialogue that's new to a space you're familiar with like Angela and Anjali did. Find people who are excited to listen or find a way to make them excited to listen. Invite them over.

What ideas do you see missing in the world? What's stopping you from bringing them to life?

THROW THE DINNER PARTY

- What do you think is missing in our conversations and ideas today? Start that new dialogue. As the instigator, you short-circuit the problem of needing an invitation.

- Reflect on the spaces you're a part of, like your industry, field of study, and hometown. What new ideas can you bring to these spaces? What ideas have you learned in these spaces that you can bring somewhere new?

- You do not need to think big to start a new conversation. If it feels intimidating, start small, like your own little corner of the internet.

- When you're starting new conversations, coin new phrases to describe your work. This will make it easier for people to process its newness.

CHAPTER 7

NOD WITH PURPOSE

———

Don't let the confines other people place on their reality restrict yours.

—AISHA BOWE

When you choose to say yes and say no can be the most consequential decision of your career.

A college student named Joe Green learned this the hard way. He and a close friend often worked on side projects together. One day, they decided to create a website called "Facemash" that asked college students to rate their peers' attractiveness.

The project got the duo in trouble with their university. Green's dad was not thrilled. "I don't think you should do anymore of these projects," he told him.

Green's friend continued to work on Facemash. When he approached Green about running the business side of the start-up, Green said no.

As the legend now goes, his friend was Mark Zuckerberg. And Facemash would soon become Facebook. If Green had said yes that day, he would have been a billionaire today. More than a decade later, he still has moments of bitterness about the fact that he said no.[110]

These kinds of stories are frustrating. Green had no way of knowing what Facebook would become. How can we decide what to say yes and no to when we know so little?

For me, this question has always been a struggle. I've had days where my Google Calendar has been filled with chaotically overlapping rectangles because I said yes to too many things and nights where I wished I'd said yes to that one golden-ticket opportunity.

The internet is wholly unhelpful when it comes to the matter. *HuffPost* and *Cosmopolitan* yell equally contradictory advice on the first page of Google. Is saying yes to everything going to change my life, or is saying no going to be the reason I finally get to sleep at night?

As with many complicated questions in life, it depends on who you ask.

When you're the underdog, the yes or no dilemma becomes even more pronounced. Saying yes to the right opportunity can be what allows your innovation to thrive. But if you say yes to too many things, you might have to say no to the perfect opportunity when it comes.

Aisha Bowe has never made a billion-dollar mistake, but she has had a lot of practice with saying yes and no at the wrong time. The conversations in which she said them at the right time changed her life.

So, what's the secret?

* * *

Aisha got on the phone with me at ten a.m. on a Saturday. I was (admittedly) still in bed, while she was making coffee and telling me about her love for furniture shopping on Wayfair.

The conversation seemed so ordinary it was easy to forget how extraordinary she was.

Aisha grew up surrounded by conflict. Her parents were divorced. Her mother cleaned houses and her father drove taxis. She assumed she could never be successful because that's what people said about children like her: children who were low-income and low-performing. It's what they said about children of color.

"I was skipping class. I was hanging out with older kids..." She trailed off. "I was doing the things you probably thought I was doing," she finished wryly.

When it came time to apply to college, Aisha applied to only one four-year school: Eastern Michigan University. She received her acceptance letter a few months later. *This is probably a mistake* was the first thought that crossed her mind. The second? *I should go to community college instead.*

At community college, she told me people assumed, "you're here because you're stupid." And she believed it. She picked the easiest major and focused on getting by and having a good time. Chasing after some arbitrary definition of success was far from her mind.

Months passed like this. On the day of an important calculus II exam, Aisha was busy getting drunk with her friends in New Orleans. It was Mardi Gras, and "yes, we were *that* kind of fun," she said, laughing.

She stumbled into her math class the next morning to take a makeup exam. It had been a long fifteen-hour trip back to school—Aisha was already counting down the minutes until she could go home and *sleep*. Her professor watched her squint-eyed as she yawned. But his eyebrows shot up when he told Aisha her score.

She had earned 100 percent on the exam.

"I really think that you should go home and think about doing something different with your life," he said.

Thinking about what to do with her life was far from her mind at that moment. All she wanted was a hot shower and some rice milk. But as her hangover wore off that day, she sat down and began to write on a piece of paper.

She wrote down the craziest things. She wrote about getting into the University of Michigan, about studying engineering, about getting a *real job*.

This new development in her story was exciting to me. "So, you were writing out your dream life," I blurted out. "You were finally saying yes."

"Kind of," she said hesitantly. "I thought of it more as 'making stuff up.' It was just so outrageous. I thought that if you don't do well in high school, you don't get to do these things."

Still, she stuck the paper on her door and tried to turn her make-believe list into reality.

Two years of math and science classes later, Aisha was reading her acceptance letter to the University of Michigan for aerospace engineering. She could hardly believe it was real.

But the battle was far from over. Aisha's classmates had many stereotypes about who she was and how she'd gotten there. "They looked at me like I was the affirmative action," Aisha told me. There were three black students in the entire aerospace program at the University of Michigan.

When Aisha tried to defend herself, her peers scowled. "You took a spot from a hard-working white man," one informed her. But after enduring so much hardship to be admitted, she had to know how wrong they were.

Right?

* * *

The perceptions people carry of us shape the way we act. This is sometimes referred to as stereotype threat: when negative stereotypes exist about us, we subconsciously confirm them through our actions. It's our mind saying yes to stereotypes without us even knowing it.[111]

In one psychology study, black and white students were split into two groups and given a test. In the first group, the psychologists told the students they were being given a problem-solving lab. In the second group, psychologists told the students they were being given a test of intellectual ability.

The results? In the first group, the black and white students performed equally well. But in the second group, the black students performed significantly worse than their peers. For the black students, being given a test of intellect evoked the stereotype they were unintelligent, leading to poorer performance.[112]

Stereotype threat influenced the way Aisha said yes and no many times. She said yes to partying instead of studying and no to Eastern Michigan University in favor of community college.

But by the time she got to the University of Michigan, she was more aware of how people's perceptions of her had shaped many of her life decisions. She was ready to threaten the stereotypes.

She worked hard at university, mastering a field she previously thought wasn't meant for people like her. Her classmates' contempt fueled her to do better. At the end of her college journey, NASA asked her the question she had never dared to dream of: would you like to work for us?

* * *

Let's go back to Facebook for a moment. During the company's early days, Joe Green was not the only one faced with consequential questions of yes and no.

Jesse Pujji was one of the platform's first users. By that time, it was no longer a place for students to rate people on their attractiveness. Facebook had evolved into a general hub for college students online. As they used the platform, Pujji and his friends had a radical idea: *what if we created Facebook for high schoolers?*

So they built. They created features for student council, club events, and school pride. They created a system to verify if their user was in high school. Answer a few questions about your high school's mascot, colors, and faculty, and the website would know if you really went there. It was radical, new, and enthralling.

When the team launched, they were overwhelmed by the number of users flowing into their systems. They worked steadily on the project for six months, trying to manage its rapid scale.

But six months in, they heard Zuckerberg was planning on expanding Facebook to high school. Intimidated by his drive and tempted by the lure of a stable job, the team left their little project to pursue corporate careers in finance. They said no.

A few years later, they discovered platforms similar to theirs exceeding valuations of $100 million. Clearly, there had been room for more than one social media network when the team had quit. "Don't quit so early," Pujji advises in a social media post, reflecting on his experience.[113] Being intimidated into saying no can cost you incredible opportunities at success.

My mother often says that "as a rule, a man is a fool." Whether it's because of competition or stereotype threat, sometimes people suck at having their own best interests at heart.

So, naturally, when Aisha got the job offer from NASA, she said no.

It was 10:33 a.m. when she told me, and I was frustrated. How *could* she? She'd been given the offer of a lifetime. It was the point in every story where things are supposed to take a turn for the better.

But this was real life. The effects of stereotype threat were more than tangible. Aisha was scared she would mess up the position. "I didn't think I deserved my achievements thus far," she said. "If I failed at the position, I would prove everyone who looked down on people like me right."

The good news is that billion-dollar government agencies hate the word "no." Plus, they have an eye for talent. The NASA recruiter persisted, inviting Aisha to an agency-wide event and showing her all the amazing people she could have worked with had she accepted the offer.

At the end of the event, he asked her what she thought. "I loved it," she admitted.

"It can all be a part of your life. Do you want the job?" At that moment, she knew she was being given a once-in-a-lifetime second chance. She said yes.

* * *

Reading Aisha's story, it probably feels easy to pinpoint the moments when she "should" have said yes and no, the times when it would have been "right" since it benefitted her life. We say yes and no to these seemingly obvious scenarios in an equally "wrong" way all the time. We don't apply to opportunities because they seem too selective. We quit working on projects because the space is too competitive. We cut ourselves short with the word "no" without even realizing it.

At the same time, when we feel we *can* do something, we say yes—far too often. Why? For one, we're scared of letting people down. In an effort to please, we're left with little bandwidth for ourselves. However, we're also bad at knowing when an opportunity is right for us. I'm often scared to say no just *in case* an opportunity ends up being transformative. As a result, I end up with way too many things to do, only a few in which I actually find value.

As Aisha found, saying "yes" at crucial times can transform your life. They can be the difference between the underdog who innovates and the underdog who's never able to. Saying yes (eventually) to NASA jumpstarted her career, but it also gave her the confidence to pursue opportunities beyond.

After six years as an aerospace engineer at the organization, Aisha decided she wanted to start a company to help minority students find their place in STEM. She'd grown up having never seen a black woman who was an engineer or an entrepreneur. She wanted to show kids that "people who looked like me could do the things that I am doing."

Aisha began with hands-on workshops that taught students about technology and entrepreneurship. She didn't have the money to do the work pro bono forever.

She did know one entity that did.

Aisha had six years of experience working at a federal agency. She knew the government's technology was lacking and they had the money to do better. So, she founded STEMBoard, a company that created software systems for both the public and private sectors. In 2020, STEMBoard was ranked as one of *Inc Magazine*'s fastest-growing private companies.[114]

STEMBoard is now a seven-figure company. As the CEO, Aisha has been able to implement innovative solutions for her clients, which include the US Department of Defense. She uses the momentum from STEMBoard to fund LINGO, an organization that distributes coding kits to students around the world, showing them the wonders of her technology. Her work has changed the lives of thousands of children. It has been featured by everyone from Kelly Clarkson to Tamron Hall.

In 2020, Aisha received the University of Michigan College of Engineering's Outstanding Recent Alumna award. The same classmates who scowled at her many years ago sent her congratulatory emails as word of the accolade spread.

Hard work and grit are important to her success, but Aisha's most crucial moments lay in saying yes and no at the right time. How can you do the same?

THE SUPPOSED TO METHOD

Let's make a list.

Take a break from reading to write down everything you did yesterday. For example, "I went for a jog. Then, I went out to eat with friends. Then, I went to a work meeting."

Once you're done, checkmark anything on your list you feel like you were "supposed" to do. In other words, there was a pressing need or obligation to do it.

Finally, look at the things you've checked, and cross off the ones you feel you did *only* because you were supposed to. In other words, if internal or external pressure didn't exist, you wouldn't have done the activities. Everything you crossed off should be your new list of things to say no to.

These are the things you do only because you feel like you *should* or *have* to. They are the things eating up your time from other, more meaningful things. They could be small things, like browsing through an online sale for a brand you dislike merely because the prices are good, or bigger things, like Aisha choosing to skip class because that's what she thought black people were "supposed" to do. Here's a snippet from my list:

Did a HIIT workout

✓ Went to an Ethiopian restaurant with my family

✓ ~~Bought clothes on sale~~

✓ Attended a work meeting

✓ ~~Went to a consulting workshop~~

Helped my dad with his LinkedIn

Wrote this chapter

What if I hadn't attended a consulting workshop because everyone else was doing it? What would I have been able to say *yes* to instead?

"It is your right to decide how you spend your time," author Tony Robbins says. "It's your right to say no."[115] To nod with purpose, you have to exercise your right to say no.

Once you begin saying *no* to things you're *only* inclined to say yes to because of pressure, you'll find yourself with a lot more time. What can you do to fill it up? Start saying *yes* to things you're *only* inclined to say no to because of pressure.

In other words, if obligation and society were figments of your imagination, you would have no problem saying yes. The only thing stopping you is it seems like something you're not supposed to do (for legal reasons, I'll add that this excludes crimes).

The Supposed To Method is about being intentional with your time. Say yes to the things that feel daring. Say no to the things that feel obligatory. As cofounder of Virgin Airlines Richard Branson declares, "If somebody offers you an amazing opportunity but you are not sure you can do it, say yes."[116] You can always learn how to do it later.

On its own, saying yes so freely can feel intimidating. How can we ensure we nod with purpose?

THE WHAT IFS METHOD

What if I got a real job?

That was the last thing on Aisha's list of "what ifs." The first step to saying yes and no at the right time is building your own.

Since elementary school, we've been told to make our goals SMART (Specific, Measurable, Achievable, Realistic, and Time-Bound).[117] A SMART goal aims for guarantees—if you put in a consistently decent amount of effort, it is guaranteed you'll achieve the goal. It is guaranteed gratification. It is *realistic*.

But the fun things in life are rarely realistic.

Growing up, my SMART goals were simple: graduate from the sixth grade, get an A in English, and convince my parents to buy me a $100 doll by my next birthday. These are the goals I wrote down. What I didn't write down were my What If goals, like directing a movie or publishing a book.

The problem with SMART goals is they limit our potential to the realm of extremely realistic possibilities. One study found only 15 percent of people believed their SMART goals would help them live up to their full potential.[118] The other 85 percent trudged through their SMART goals merely because they seemed more realistic.

SMART goals aren't all bad. They just need to be used in conjunction with something else: What If goals. What If goals are big, vague, and grand. Writing them down feels daring, even intimidating. Once you have your What If goals written down, you can write down your SMART *steps*. Goals represent endpoints that are grand, but steps can be concrete and time-bound. SMART steps are getting an A in math and pursuing an aerospace engineering degree. They're the things that get you to your What If goals.

Deciding when to say yes and no starts with the question, can this help me take a step toward my What If?

For Aisha, her SMART goal was graduating from community college with an easy major. Her What If goal was becoming an aerospace engineer. Once she wrote her What If goals down and began looking at them every morning, she began saying yes to "what if?" instead of "what's practical?"

Start with the question, what if I could _____? Now go on and fill in the blanks.

* * *

Many cultures around the world developed independently of each other. Still, there are remarkable similarities among them. Almost every culture, for example, eats rice in some form. They nod their heads up and down to say "yes." Why?

It's a strange phenomenon that has gotten everyone from Charles Darwin to modern-day scientists scratching their heads. The simplest theory is that nodding is like a stunted bow.[119] It is a mark of submission; an agreement to accept what is being said.

But not all nods are created equal. In South Asia, people often opt for a vaguer gesture instead, creating a side-to-side arc with their heads. Academics call it the head bobble or the Indian head shake. One writer describes it as "somewhat like an infinity sign, or a numeral eight lying down."[120] It can mean anything from *yes, of course* to *I am pretending to agree to spare your feelings.*

It's hard to innovate when you always say "yes" as a head bobble instead of a nod. While you would only submit to things that strongly exemplify your values, you can vaguely agree with much more.

If the elaborate methods in this chapter ever overwhelm you or you face a pivotal yes-no question, just think of "yes" as a firm nod. You want to nod with purpose. You want to nod with *your purpose in mind.*

I imagine now Aisha Bowe, Joe Green, and Jesse Pujji would all tell me the same thing if I asked them about the secret to cracking the yes-no question: it's more complicated than it seems. The words yes and no dictate how we spend our time, but they also reflect larger truths about our values and potential to fulfill our dreams. They can be the difference between living life self-destructively and working for NASA; between making hundreds of dollars and billions.

So, say yes like a proud bow. Say no politely but directly. Know what you deserve. Accept nothing less. Maybe shake up some government agencies while you're at it.

NOD WITH PURPOSE

- The ways people perceive us influence the things we say yes and say no to. Write down a list of perceptions people have of you. Are you subconsciously conforming to them?

- Make a list of everything you did today. What are the things you did *only* because you were supposed to? These are the things you should say no to.

- Reflect on all the things you decide not to do every day. Which ones are you avoiding *only* because you think you aren't supposed to do them? Start saying yes to them.

- Create a list of big What If goals: lofty and thrilling. Then, write down the SMART (Specific, Measurable, Achievable, Realistic, and Time-Bound) steps you need to take to achieve those goals. Prioritize saying yes to opportunities that help you take SMART steps.

- When you feel especially stuck about whether to say yes or no, think of nodding like a bow. Is the activity in question something you would be proud to submit to? Does it exemplify your values?

CHAPTER 8

TUG ON THE STRING

———

*When you empathize and understand where someone is coming
from, you can explain new ideas and opportunities to them.*

—ALFONSO COBO

Let's do an exercise.

I will give you three words and you have to find one word
relating to all of them. For example, if I gave you the words
"manner," "round," and "tennis," you could say table. Table
manners are important for politeness. Table tennis is a common sport. Round table discussions are common in academia.

Now it's your turn. If you have a pencil and paper nearby, try
writing the words down and thinking about them carefully.
Your words are "wise," "work," and "tower." Give yourself two
minutes to brainstorm an answer. Write down the word you
come up with. We'll get to the answer soon.

I never asked him this question, but I think Alfonso Cobo
would get it correct.

He grew up in the bustling streets of Madrid, Spain. An intro-
vert in a city of never-ending chatter, he often felt like he was

battling two sides of himself: the one he wanted to show to the world and the one that was really him.

"I started going out pretty early on and hung out with kids I shouldn't have hung out with," he said. "I hid many of my interests or passions because I was afraid to show how much of a 'weirdo' or 'nerd' I really was."

It didn't help that Alfonso is gay. "There's a certain pressure that comes with your image, being gay in the city," he told me. "It's about where you hang out and who you hang out with." People were paying attention to what he did, so Alfonso humored them. He pretended to be "normal."

But on his own, he was exploring. He observed the way design breathed life through Madrid. He observed people. He didn't have much to say to them, but that meant he was always listening.

On one yellow-sand beach in Málaga, he recounts bumping into a boy who was stuttering through Spanish. As he tried to understand his words, Alfonso realized the boy was a Syrian refugee who had experienced some of the worst horrors in the world. The boy had barely made it into Spain. Alfonso could feel the goosebumps rising on his skin.

It was here, among Málaga's waves, that Alfonso first understood the power of stories. But can stories help you innovate?

* * *

Still have your response to the puzzle from the beginning of the chapter? The answer was "clock." Many iconic buildings are clock*towers*. We can take turns for a game going clock*wise*. A factory assembly line can run like clock*work*.

This question is an example of the Remote Associates Test, which assesses the cognitive abilities that underlie creative thinking. If you found the test difficult, you're not alone. If you got to the right answer, you likely have higher-than-average creativity.[121]

Or you're experiencing a healthy dose of beginner's luck.

In one Columbia University study that used the Remote Associates Test, participants were split into two groups. One group was asked to reflect on their experiences dating someone from another country. The other group was asked to reflect on their experiences dating someone from the same country.

The first group far outperformed the second group on the test.[122] When we reflect on stories that diverge from our own, our brains are better primed for creativity.

The study from Columbia paid particular attention to romantic relationships, but similar outcomes have been observed in many intimate intercultural experiences—from living abroad to forming close friendships with someone from a different background.[123]

Being able to understand people who have life experiences different from our own is a powerful tool for innovation, but it can also feel lofty. How can we concretely better understand people? Alfonso's solution was to seek stories.

In 2016, Alfonso was accepted into the Parsons School of Design in America.[124] They offered him a huge scholarship. It was just enough to be affordable.

He came to New York with some spare change for food and basic necessities in his pocket. In his last year at school, as he looked for job opportunities, he realized there was no way for him to easily show his design work to employers. He wanted to create a better way to tell his story.

Alfonso didn't know how to code, so his dad agreed to lend him five hundred dollars to hire a developer. Over the next few months, Alfonso's mini-project evolved into an app that provided curated, aesthetically pleasing social media story templates. He called it Unfold.

As Alfonso spent more and more of his time on Unfold, his parents began to get cold feet. They were begging their son to get a real job. "They found it really hard to understand what I was doing," Alfonso said.

It's hard to blame them. Alfonso often found himself turning to his friends for money. Sometimes, it was just for a meal that was not boiled pasta.

Money was tight. App engagement was low. Alfonso's parents were desperate. What was left?

* * *

In 2013, seventeen-year-old Kal Turnbull observed that his friends only seemed to care about three things: *Breaking Bad*, Scottish independence, and indie rock. Turnbull wasn't ready to protest "punk is not dead" with them.

"In the grand scheme of the world, we all thought similarly," he said. "This led me to wonder, what does someone actually do when they want to hear a different perspective?"

This question spurred him to launch "Change My View," a subreddit where people could go to have their minds changed.[125] In seven years, the subreddit has amassed over one million members.[126]

If you have an opinion, you can post it on the subreddit. Posting is a commitment—when the floodgates of comments open, you have to respond to each one within three hours. If someone manages to change your mind or even a nuance in your view, you can award them a delta-shaped symbol next to their username.[127]

As I read through responses on the page, most of them seemed to be at least two paragraphs long, filled with stories and personal experiences. Discourse was not only thoughtful but also polite. It was an indicator of what modern-day Congress *should* look like.

If you're itching to open your laptop and see the community for yourself, be warned: it's a deep rabbit hole to tumble down.

Change My View makes up a small fraction of the internet. It's a testament to the power of listening. By enforcing the three-hour rule and removing dismissive comments, Turnbull forces people who post their opinions to listen to opposing views. When we listen carefully to others' stories, it can change the trajectory of our own.

Listening helps us understand people better and stretches our minds. Writer William Arthur Ward once said, "If you can imagine it, you can create it."[128] When we listen, we give our minds more possibilities to imagine. This gives us more things we can create.

Listening is a superpower and it was all Alfonso had left.

The question that remained: would it be enough?

* * *

On Instagram, I get daily message requests from creators asking me to try their apps, services, and products. I've responded to roughly zero of them.

In the early days of Unfold, Alfonso's strategy for getting customers was similar: send cold direct messages. The difference? Alfonso got responses from nearly 50 percent.

As he explained, "In this very superficial world, we really want genuine human connection." Alfonso knew how to create that genuine connection with people. He had been listening to them for years.

One influencer he messaged was @earth, an Instagram account with one million followers. The account was owned by twenty-three-year-old Andy McCune. His stories looked exactly like Unfold's, with one key difference: it took Andy a dozen minutes longer to create them.

If someone told me they could save me a dozen minutes every day for free, I would begin daydreaming about the additional cup of coffee I could make myself with the new-found time. Andy was no different. After he tried out the app, he eagerly began asking Alfonso questions about his future business plans.

The two met in a small coffee shop in New York. "I knew that I needed help if I wanted Unfold to become bigger," Alfonso told me. Andy had experience with social media. Alfonso had the intuition of people. "I felt that he [Andy] was the piece I was missing." When Alfonso asked Andy to be his cofounder, Andy said yes.

If you've ever wondered how much influencers on social media have paid to create aesthetic stories, it's probably zero dollars. The magic behind their effortless aesthetic? Unfold. Today, everyone from Selena Gomez to Tommy Hilfiger to Kim Kardashian uses the app to create well-designed online content.

Unfold was acquired by website-building giant Squarespace a year after it was founded by Alfonso and Andy. Yet, before the acquisition, Alfonso spent zero dollars on marketing. He didn't need to. Unfold connected with users through stories.

Even as part of a corporation like Squarespace, the product operates on intuition. Market research is rarely considered necessary. The team doesn't bother—they know Alfonso *gets* people.

As a strategy for innovation, listening to others' stories sounds easy enough. The problem is that most people overestimate their listening abilities. The average person only listens at about 25 percent efficiency.[129] There are more fascinating stories out there than people who can listen to and treasure them.

How can we optimize our listening?

BE A NARRATOR

I'll admit it.

Sometimes, when I'm listening to someone talk, I'm practicing what I want to say next in my head. In all my efforts to amaze the person I'm talking to with my next line, I barely hear what they're saying.

One Princeton University study compared brain activity in a speaker and a listener. It found there is a significant delay between the moment we hear something and the moment we understand it. On average, it took the listener's brain one to four seconds to mirror the speaker's. That's how long it would take you to speak this sentence. For some, the delay was a minute long.[130]

It's not that we don't have the capacity to listen. Most people speak at a rate of 175-200 words a minute. Our brain processes 600-1,000 words a minute.[131] If our brain processes information so much quicker than people speak, why are we still slow to listen?

When the Princeton researchers dug deeper, they found another part of the listener's brain that was *preceding* the speaker's. In other words, the listener was anticipating what the speaker was going to say before they actually said it. We are slow to listen because it takes us time to reconcile what we actually hear with what we expect.[132]

This kind of anticipation is helpful when conversations are predictable. If the speaker is saying something entirely novel, some of that novelty is lost in our internal dialogue. We fall prey to confirmation bias, interpreting what we hear in a way that conforms to what we expect the speaker to say.[133] Imagine how much beauty and nuance in conversation we miss out on every day.

How can we keep ourselves focused on what people are saying? How can we bridge the gap between the speed of our brain and the speed of their speech?

The problem is we want to add our own internal judgments and ideas to the things we hear. The solution is to train our minds back on the external. As you listen to someone talk, repeat what you're hearing verbatim in your mind. Make the inner voice in your head a narrator—its job is to be as accurate as possible.

By giving your mind a task as it listens to someone talk, you can fill up the seconds it would have ordinarily spent wandering.

This kind of careful listening doesn't just make you a better person. It is crucial for innovation.

Doug Augustine's father bought a Taco Bell store with his entire life savings. Through the labor of second jobs and love, the store survived and grew. Augustine's dad quickly went from one store to seven, the first franchisee at the time to do so.

But his finances could not justify the rapid expansion. The stress took a toll on him. Augustine's dad passed away from a heart attack, leaving his son with a business that was falling apart.

Augustine wanted to revive the company. Taco Bell headquarters was not optimistic. "You're in a death spiral," they told him. "You cannot pull this off." Augustine looked at the community his father had spent so many years building and knew he could not let them down.

He asked them questions. "What is the biggest problem you're facing right now?" he asked employees. "How can we better serve you?" he asked their customers.

Then, he listened. He listened to learn rather than to respond. His goal wasn't to impress them or assert his authority as the new CEO—he just wanted to understand what had gone wrong. Slowly, things began to turn around.[134]

When I spoke to him, Augustine had quadrupled his father's business to twenty-eight stores. The Taco Bell COO presented him with the company's Flying Pig Award. His probability of success had been as likely as pigs flying. "You don't have to start big to achieve the impossible," he told me. "You just have to commit to listening to one person every day."

When you focus on listening for the sake of listening, you're better equipped to understand an issue and innovate on it. But is there a point to practicing this throughout your life?

START WITH ABUNDANCE

It's easier to assemble a stunning bouquet if you start in a botanical garden. It's easier to create something new if you start with abundance.

Online creator and entrepreneur David Perell talks about the importance of this in respect to writing: "Instead of creating new information, you organize the information you already have."[135] He believes if you take good notes on all the things you learn, you will never run out of ideas to build upon.

Innovation works in a similar way. Instead of information, your building blocks are stories.

Unfold has now expanded beyond Instagram templates. They're on their way to becoming the go-to app for creating aesthetic social media content. Throughout our conversation, I asked Alfonso a few times what he attributed to all his successes and continuous creativity, but he never seemed to give me a straightforward answer. I was flustered.

"I guess I've always been a good listener," he said one time. He began telling me about the stories he remembers of people he has encountered. Though it has been over a decade since he has talked to some of them, it felt like he was telling me about people he met yesterday.

Alfonso *was* being straightforward. He was just giving me an answer I wasn't ready to hear. I wanted him to tell me I could seek inspiration in three easy steps. But stories and people are where he finds inspiration, and he is not the only one.

One entrepreneur I spoke with has letters of stories from people who have been touched by his company posted in his office. Stories give his team a reason to keep creating. Entrepreneur and author James Clear keeps more than seventeen books on his desks when he writes. If he gets stuck, he reads.[136]

In my realm of more everyday projects, I recently realized I've been collecting stories my whole life. My mother always laughs when she speculates how much worse my memory can get by the time I'm eighty. I have some of the worst memory in my family, including my grandparents, so I grew up writing down all the random stories I heard.

This chapter gave me some of the worst writer's block I have ever had; I was very close to missing my manuscript deadline. As I desperately flipped through ideas and sat hungrily at local cafés, I decided to pore over my story notes for the first time in years. It helped me see connections between ideas I never would have in the moment—and it helped keep my publisher happy.

When you're the underdog, innovation is intimidating. You may not have as many mentors or resources to guide you. You may not even have an idea. Listening is about bridging the gap. When you collect other people's stories and experiences, you're never starting from scratch—you're starting from abundance.

✷ ✷ ✷

Innovation happens when you listen. Far too often, precious words get lost.

Back in the day (circa 1600), one of the biggest barriers to listening was geography. There were no smartphones for your friend's face to magically appear on while she walked around the other side of the world.

When words would get lost in distance, people used string. String helped guide people's words to their end destination. One person would speak into it, and the words would travel through the string into the ear of the listener waiting on the other end.[137]

Soon, people began attaching cups to each end of the string. Romantics claim it is because people have an "irrepressible urge to press shells to our ears, to hear the still-surviving echo of the world's first expression."[138] Scientists claim it makes it easier to actually hear things.

Whichever side of the spectrum you're on, it was an inefficient way to communicate. People would strain their ears just to catch a whisper of the speaker's words. If they really wanted to pay attention, they would tug on the string. The tauter it was, the better the sound traveled.[139]

While we've since been blessed with the telephone, listening is just as active a process now as it was then to be effective. For the underdog, effective listening is key for successful innovation.

Strain your ears, press the cup a little closer, and tug on the string. What stories do you hear?

TUG ON THE STRING

- Stories spark creativity when they challenge your ways of thinking. Think about how you currently meet new people. Are their stories generally different from your own? If not, where can you seek out different stories? Consider local groups, nearby shops, and online communities.

- Humans are naturally bad listeners. In order to understand others' stories, you have to make an active effort to listen when someone is speaking. When you're having a conversation, try narrating the person's speech in your mind to keep yourself focused on what they're saying.

- Stories are the building blocks of innovation. Note down stories when you meet people. Then, you'll never start creative work from scratch.

CHAPTER 9

BE THE PEACOCK

———

You can turn a shoelace into a global movement. You can do anything.

—DANIEL KASIDI

I was six years old and lost.

I remember calling out for help and hearing the buzz of an indifferent, impatient crowd moving through their Black Friday shopping in response. The challenges of being four feet tall inside a mall of giants are plenty, but the most significant one is being noticed.

I needed someone to pause from their day long enough to help me find my parents. As the crowd continued to move impassively, one thing was clear to me: speaking louder would not be enough. How could I catch people's attention?

Lemon-lime-flavored Kool-Aid might have some answers. A study conducted by the University of California, San Diego asked participants to pour and drink from a pitcher of the juice. Some participants were shown pictures of either happy or angry faces. Others were shown either positive or negative words (think "wedding" vs. "knife").

The scientists found the people shown pictures of happy faces drank significantly more Kool-Aid than those shown angry faces. For the people who were shown words, there was no significant change in Kool-Aid consumption based on the kind of word they were shown.[140]

As I discovered at six years old, words can be powerful, but they are often not powerful enough to change our behavior.

It's why things would have been different at the mall that day if I was a peacock, strutting through the shops in all my blue-and-green feathered glory. I wouldn't have to be heard—I would be seen.

Similarly, for the underdog, speaking louder to get people to take notice of our work is just not enough. We hear cries for help every day on the news from countries around the world, and it is all too easy to turn off the TV. Seeing the images of the crisis on social media makes our hearts drop and sends our brains racing to take action.[141]

To catch people's attention and spark change with our ideas, we need to be seen. We need to be the peacock.

But how?

* * *

The first thing I noticed about Daniel Kasidi was his charisma. The second thing I noticed was his appreciation for the intricacies of English.

"Where do you seek inspiration?" I asked him once we'd settled into our call.

He paused. "It depends. Do you mean *seek* or *find*?"

Stumped, I let him choose. His answer was effortlessly eloquent.

Daniel spent the first five years of his life in Kenya. "Everyone looked like me there," he recounts. "Community was different." He would play outside with the other kids while his parents went to work. People shared with open arms and treated each other like family.

But when he came to America, he didn't fit in so seamlessly. His classmates made fun of his accent and his heritage. "All they knew of Africa was what they saw on National Geographic," Daniel explained to me. He didn't speak English at the time, so he couldn't tell them any better.

Daniel ended up spending most of his time at home with his siblings. "We were so ashamed of our language, Swahili, because we got ridiculed so much," he admitted to me. "We wanted to forget it, so we just spoke English with each other." The words he glides through now are the same words he once stumbled on.

Immigrant children like Daniel make up a quarter of all children in America.[142] Still, they have a significantly higher chance of being bullied at school.[143]

Why? Psychologists believe it's because kids are insecure.[144] They crave the power rush they get from alienating kids different from them. Immigrant children, with their distinct accents, make the perfect target.

I grew up in an immigrant-dominated school, though I would hesitate to call us diverse. We had many students who were of South Asian descent. The outsiders happened to be the few non-Asian kids we did have. We bonded over our common experiences as minorities, blasting both Bollywood music and R&B at prom. Who were the most common victims of bullying?

It wasn't the non-Asian kids. It was the immigrants. How could immigrants be the outsiders in a school filled with people like them?

Bullies targeted the kids who seemed the most "immigrant-like." In practice, this meant the kids who stumbled over English or didn't speak at all. As a result, these students were rarely befriended. They were not seen because their accents were all people heard. Even when we all looked the same, people alienated the students based on how they spoke.

Daniel Kasidi was forced to understand how unfairly America treats immigrants early on, so he set out to do the opposite: he wanted to be seen *without* being heard. The question that remained was how?

While the kids around him watched Bruce Lee and Jackie Chan movies with wonder, Daniel watched them with a purpose. He wanted to learn their art.

From the ages of eight to thirteen, when Daniel came home from school, he observed videos and mimicked what he saw. Each day, he stretched, somersaulted, and held stances for four hours.

When his parents saved enough money to afford karate classes, Daniel was already prepared for his black belt, the highest level you can achieve in the sport.[145] He didn't need to tell the karate master anything—his skill spoke for itself.

After mastering karate, Daniel moved onto skateboarding, spending hours practicing at a local park. His tricks looked cool, and the people around him began to take notice. By the time he got to high school, he had found his place among friends who shared his love for the sport. They barely remembered the withdrawn, stuttering Daniel from years back.

Being the peacock helped Daniel find belonging in a new country. Though he was still introverted, he was comfortable speaking English with his new friends. He felt accepted. Maybe being the peacock wouldn't matter so much anymore.

* * *

America has an entirely irrational obsession with Apple.

Admittedly, I say this typing away on my MacBook Air while my iPhone buzzes with notifications. Still, it's true. Let's take laptops as an example.

The price of the latest Microsoft Surface Pro starts at $749.99. The price of the latest MacBook Pro is almost 70 percent higher, starting at $1,299. Website after website consistently declares the two similar in terms of features.[146] But Apple holds 15 percent of the PC market in America, while Microsoft gets a measly 5 percent.[147]

Even worse, Apple seems nonchalant with its product launches. As one *IndustryWeek* journalist expresses with frustration, Apple has a tradition of not talking much about devices soon to be released. On the other hand, its competitors' plans for the future "are much more specific, and there are real products attached to them."[148]

Their innovation is heard. Apple's is seen.

I still remember the dopamine that rushed to my brain when I opened my first MacBook. Though it was technically owned by my school district, something about the unboxing experience was thrilling. I remember lifting the top of the crisp, stark white box and sliding my new laptop neatly out. The silver Apple logo gleamed.

Apple is the peacock. The company dramatically unveils new features at their long-anticipated annual conferences, while rival companies tell the media excitedly about their plans months in advance. In a world with so much noise about innovation and entrepreneurship, peacocks have the edge in sparking delight.

It is a truth Daniel would soon discover too. It was his senior year of high school and he was waiting for his friend to pick him up. *This guy is taking forever.*

As he sat and waited, tapping his foot, he began playing around with some spare shoelaces. Eventually, his fidgeting formed a bracelet. When his friend finally arrived, Daniel slipped it on his wrist and thought little of it.

But his friend noticed and was impressed, asking him eagerly if Daniel could make him one too.

The next day, more and more of Daniel's friends had the same question when they saw his new bracelet: can I get one?

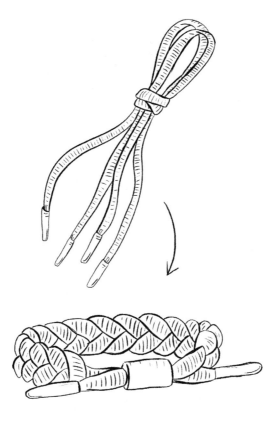

A sketch of Daniel's shoelace bracelet.

Daniel could sense he was on the brink of something interesting with these bracelets, but he didn't know he was holding the potential for an entire global movement in his hands.

After the shoelace incident, Daniel went to college and worked in fashion at companies like Levi's and Reebok. That bracelet and the looks of delight on his friends' faces were always at the back of his mind. Could it have been something bigger? "I just didn't want to live with that question mark in my life," he told me.

It was 2010. The economy was still reeling from the effects of the Great Recession. "It had been thirty-six months with the economy kind of in the dumps," American labor and workplace journalist Steven Greenhouse described.[149] People were dejected. Hope for the future was waning.

In a time when things seemed so uncertain, Daniel left stability to start a company. He called it Rastaclat. Investors were heavily leaning toward technology companies at the time, which seemed like safer investments. A company selling shoelace bracelets was an outlier in every way. He needed a miracle.

Daniel went with three words instead: Seek the Positive.

It was the brand's slogan, embedded into each bracelet Rastaclat made. In a time of unease, each bracelet was a symbol of hope. Among the sea of technology corporations, Rastaclat was the peacock. It stood out without having to speak the language of the status quo.

Today, Rastaclat bracelets are found on wrists everywhere, from immigrant children to athletes in the NBA and Olympics. By doing what he did best and being the peacock, Daniel has brought smiles and changed lives.

What's the secret?

FAN OUT YOUR FEATHERS

Indie game *Among Us* was created in June of 2018. Each player is privately given a role at the beginning of the game: crewmate or impostor. The crewmates scuttle across a ship to complete a set of tasks. The impostors try to kill the crewmates without getting caught. At the end of each round, all the players discuss who they think the impostor is and vote to have the person eliminated. It's a game of collaboration and survival.

Among Us was greeted with little enthusiasm when it was first released, as most indie games are. But by November 2020, the game had over 500 million active players.[150] What happened?

There's a popular claim circulating the conversation around innovation that our attention spans are getting shorter. Specifically, people say the average human attention span is eight seconds. A goldfish's attention span is nine seconds.

The only problem? The claim is false.

Many psychologists have now spoken out against the theory. "There is no real evidence that it's [the human attention span] changed since it was first reported in the late 1800s," Dr. Michael Posner, a scientist who works with the brain networks underlying attention, says.[151] In fact, if you're still here reading this book, you've probably outperformed your average carnival goldfish.

One thing, however, is changing: the number of ideas available to us. On Twitter alone, more than 500 million tweets are published every day in 2021, which translates to an average of 5,787 tweets per second.[152] To get people interested in our work, we need to catch their attention immediately. Otherwise, they have 5,786 more ideas they can consider instead with the swipe of a finger.

The good news is everyone has something about them that's awe-worthy. For peacocks, it's their large, brightly colored feathers. For *Among Us*, it was its social aspect. "There's more natural conversation that arises from it," *Internet Today* writer Ricky Hayberg, explains. "It's more of a party game. You're kind of just hanging out with friends and the game is secondary."[53]

In early 2020, the coronavirus pandemic hit. People were forced to stay at home and quarantine. As a result, many video gamers began playing the game live online. Viewers saw how enthusiastically the streamers were discussing the game with each other—*Among Us* was fanning out its feathers.

In a world of regular, in-person socializing, *Among Us* was a pigeon. In a quarantined world, *Among Us* was the peacock. The game's popularity skyrocketed.

You may not know what your feathers are yet, but you also have something about you impossible to miss. It doesn't need to revolutionize popular culture or start a global movement— it just needs to get people to pay attention.

A couple months ago, I took a business class that started at the inhumanely early hour of eight in the morning. I had already resolved to spend at least half of the class napping.

But on the first day, the professor showed up wearing a turtle onesie. Needless to say, he had my attention. His feathers were not the costume itself. Rather, they were his unabashedly calm face as he talked to us dressed as a turtle. His confidence made me want to pay attention. He was impossible to nap over.

To be heard, you have to be seen. To be seen, you have to fan out your feathers. Once you are seen, what do people hear?

SHAKE YOUR TAIL

I spoke to Daniel on a week when I had three exams and a manuscript deadline. I was tired, but his call felt rejuvenating. Having grown up stumbling through English, he cherishes words more than anyone I have ever met. His words were razor sharp. His speech was pointed. His ideas were concentrated—each word communicated more.

I hung up the phone feeling ready to take on the world.

Humans are programmed to speak. A lot. Our brain treats communication as a crucial survival tool. Our favorite subject? Ourselves.[154] One study even found that people were willing to pay money to talk about themselves.[155]

In a world of self-centered noise, delivering concentrated value to other people is powerful. As underdogs, it is even more important. We cannot cut through the noise with brute force—buying advertisements, leveraging high-profile connections, or leaning on others' work. With limited resources, we have to be strategic.

For innovation to succeed, it needs support. We can get that support by being laser-focused with our words. Consider your mission. What is the driving purpose of your work? It could be to serve the underestimated or to transform the way people do an everyday task.

Daniel's mission is to inspire. "I want to scale positivity," he told me fervently. "I want to apply that feeling of hope by the billions." Rastaclat's brand speaks to that with its slogan, Seek the Positive. Three words and it's all you need to know. It makes you want to support Daniel. It is exactly enough.

Peacocks make sounds by shaking their tails, but the sound is so low-pitched that humans can't hear it. If a peacock ever were to make an audible noise, the whole world would lean in to listen. Do you make it worth people's time when they lean in for you?

* * *

I used to think of conversations in zigzags. Someone talks. I listen. I talk. They listen. Repeat. Repeat. Repeat.

In reality, conversations are three-dimensional. Getting people to engage involves nonverbal cues to catch attention. The way we present ourselves and our ideas shapes the way people listen to our words.

As underdogs, we are often the misfits in the spaces we engage in. If we embrace that, we can be the peacocks in our everyday conversations. The more people take notice of us, the easier it is to share our ideas and innovate.

Now let's get back to the question I asked Daniel at the beginning of this chapter. "Where do you seek inspiration?"

"My inspiration starts with the question: 'how can I inspire people?'" he told me. "How do I take the little Daniel who was so afraid to speak and was eventually able to accomplish all this and bring someone else like that out of his shell? I want to tell people that you can turn a shoelace into a global movement. You can do anything."

It was my first question to him and my first time hearing him talk. There was a long pause after he finished. "Did the Wi-Fi go out?" he asked me, bewildered.

"Nope, I'm still here," I responded quickly. I remember smiling to myself. I could not *wait* for the rest of this interview.

Be intentional as you converse. How can you emanate those impossible-to-miss brightly colored green and blue feathers?

BE THE PEACOCK

- Conversations are three-dimensional. To catch people's attention and spark change with your ideas, you have to be seen.

- Reflect on your strengths. What is the one thing about you that's awe-worthy? How can you ensure it comes through when you're engaging in conversation?

- Once people pay attention to you, you have to make it worth their time to listen. Take time to reflect on your values and driving mission. Stick them on your wall and channel them when you are speaking.

- Aim to provide concentrated value with your words. Be mindful of people's time by communicating value succinctly.

PART III

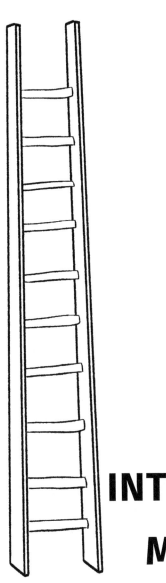

INTENTIONAL

MOVEMENT

CHAPTER 10

KNOCK ON THE DOOR

The best things in life have no clear path to them.

—ALI ABDAAL

I'll be honest.

I have no idea how to open the window in my room. There's a screen I can never seem to get past and many stray bolts whose purpose I don't know. The comforting thing about windows is there are no surprises once you manage to budge one open—apart from the occasional bee coming too close for comfort.

Doors are the opposite. While it's easy to bring your hand up and knock, there's a lot of doubt about what you'll find behind the door. Who will open it? What will the other side look like? Will the door even open? It's a low-effort, high-uncertainty activity. According to Ali Abdaal, what's hiding behind those doors are often the best opportunities.

I discovered Ali when he was knocking on YouTube's door back in 2017. At the time, he didn't know if it would swing open for him.

Over three hundred hours of content was being uploaded to the platform each minute.[156] His competition was stiff. His probability of success was low.

Uncertainty is intrinsic to doors. Most doors never open to anything fruitful. By 2017, Ali had been posting on YouTube for two years and was averaging a humble twenty thousand views per video. With YouTubers earning about four dollars per one thousand views, he was nowhere close to earning a living.[157]

How could he know if it was worth it to keep going?

* * *

Think big.

In a society that thrives on scale, it's something we hear often. So we do. We chase after the next big thing and dream about how to make small ideas blow up and beg the powers that be for *more, please.* But in our obsession with big, we overlook an entire class of innovators: the microentrepreneurs of the passion economy.

These are the people who write our favorite newsletters or the ones we follow on Instagram for fashion inspiration. They scale businesses exponentially by capitalizing on their skills. Their product is their own individuality. They run a one-person show that can make millions.

"Users can now build audiences at scale and turn their passions into livelihoods," passion economy pioneer Li-Jin explains.[158] In a world where technology is becoming ubiquitous, the passion economy is exciting because anyone can open up their laptop and try to create wealth.

Increasingly, many people are. Over 700,000 artists sell art on digital marketplace Redbubble.[159] More than 200,000 creators use Patreon, a platform on which they can charge fans for content.[160] Success is reserved for an elite few. Only 2 percent of Patreon creators earn at least federal minimum wage.[161] Everyone in the passion economy starts as the underdog. To stand out, you have to innovate.

To maximize your chances of innovation, you have to knock on every door you can.

Though he didn't realize it at the time, Ali had been knocking on doors since he was a gangly teenager growing up in England. "In high school, my whole identity was based around trying to come top of the year," he recounted. He was the kind of kid who probably complained every time he got a ninety-five. His eyes were set on the top universities in the country.

Ali quickly realized academics were draining when your entire identity depended on them. He wasn't ready to give up on earning the world record for most letter As on a single page, but he needed other things to engage his attention.

Ali discovered the joy of side projects. He taught himself to code. He set up his own website-designing agency. He learned about music. "I focused my time on the interesting things that I could get reasonably good at, but not strive to be world-class," he explained. His goal was to diversify his identity.

"It's very doable to get into the top 10 percent in most fields, without actually putting in too much time and effort," he mused. "But to get into the top 1 percent of most fields, you have to make it your whole life." After spending years thinking he had to devote his life to being the best, shooting for just the top 10 percent was thrilling.

Trying new things helped Ali deal with academic stress. For the rest of us, can we truly justify chasing opportunities that have no clear reward?

* * *

Depending on where you are in the world, you might call the old children's prank *Knock Knock Ginger, Chappy,* or *Ding Dong Ditch*. Each variation involves a similar drill: knock on someone's front door and then run before they get the chance to open it.

The origin of the game is just as hotly debated as its name. Most likely, the prank originated from an old British poem:

> *Ginger, Ginger broke a winder*
> *Hit the winda—Crack!*
> *The baker came out to give 'im a clout.*
> *And landed on his back.*[162]

Growing up, the joy of the game was in craning my neck from behind a bush to watch my neighbor peer outside in bewilderment. The goal was always to get them to open the door.

The thing with pranks is you have to work your way up to good ones. If I dared you to *Ding Dong Ditch* Bill Gates right now, you would probably shake your head vehemently. If we were childhood friends who had been playing the prank on our neighbors for years, you might be slightly more inclined to agree.

Whether you're trying to irk a billionaire or build something new, knocking on small doors makes it easier to knock on bigger ones.

Ali was approaching his last year of high school, which meant it was time for him to face the dreaded existential question: what would he do with the rest of his life?

University in the UK is traditionally three years. Ali had taught himself how to code, so computer science seemed like the natural choice for his degree. "But six years at university seemed much more interesting than three," he told me.

That left him with one option. Ali decided to study medicine.

One of the medical admissions exams he had to take was called the BMAT. Despite having a high tolerance for studying, he found that preparing for the BMAT was awful. The exam resources available were subpar at best and expensive at worst.

Ali was accepted into Cambridge University's medical school in 2012. His childhood dreams had come to fruition. He was grateful, but he wanted to create a better studying experience for future university applicants.

He wasn't the first to have noticed the problems with the BMAT. "It was not a noble idea at all," he said. "Everyone has this idea when they get into med school. They think, 'I want to help other kids get into med school.'"

One thing he had that everyone else didn't? Ten years of website design and coding knowledge.

It was 2013, and website templates were more than a few easy clicks away. For most people, creating pretty websites was completely out of reach. Ali got one up and running within a few days.

It was a collaboration between him and five other friends. They called their medical exam preparation company 6med. "It was really hard to imagine that 6med could be successful," Ali admitted. After all, every vaguely entrepreneurial medical student across the UK had seemingly tried to create the same company.

Still, Ali was excited about the opportunity to pick up a few new skills and maybe knock some doors down.

"What was your favorite memory from building 6med?" I asked him.

He paused for a couple of seconds before grinning. "We were running a course in Imperial College London and we had thirty students ready for it," he recalled. "We got to the venue with all of our boxes and books and the room we were supposed to use was locked." Rooms were locked by default on the weekend, and the janitor had forgotten about the team's room booking.

"Our students were freezing in the cold outside, probably thinking, 'this is so unprofessional.'" He laughed. "It turned into a wild goose chase of running around campus trying to convince anyone we could find to let us in."

Memories like these made Ali's eyes light up as we talked. Business was not as glamorous as he thought it would be, but that was what made it fun.

Eventually, one of the staff people relented and opened the door.

Two years later, Ali and his team were baffled by how to manage the immense interest 6med had received. They'd gone from 100 students in England to thirty-two thousand globally. By treating the experience as a door with no clear reward on the other side, Ali never thought to plan for success. "It wasn't the worst business problem to have," he told me coyly.

Doors are like dominoes. When one swings open, it often has another door behind it. Small, trapdoor-sized doors swing open to bigger, better doors. For Ali, the door of website design that he knocked on many years ago had opened to reveal another door behind it: a successful entrepreneurial venture. To maximize your own chances of knocking on a door with a bigger door behind it, you have to knock on many small doors.

DOORS ARE
LIKE DOMINOES

So, which way to the nearest trapdoor?

✳ ✳ ✳

All of my dad's favorite stories to tell start with "back in the day."

"Back in the day, we wouldn't text people before going to their house," he says. "We would just show up."

The difference between him and a robber? My dad would always knock.

When I make plans, I have many layers of permission to peel through. I ask the person, follow up over text, ping-pong back and forth until we find a time, and then confirm the day before. For my dad, merely knocking on someone's door was how he used to ask for permission.

While I will never understand my dad's method for real-life interactions, it applies perfectly to metaphorical doors. In fact, "never ask for permission" was the first piece of advice Ali gave me during our call.

In a system where you are often working under other people's rules, doing something on your own can feel disorienting. "We default to thinking that someone needs to give us per-mission to do the thing we have to do," Ali explains. "But if I had emailed the university's marketing team and said, 'Hey, is it okay to run this course?' they probably would have said no, even though there was no real risk for them."

When you're knocking on doors, permission shouldn't cross your mind. You can always ask for forgiveness later.

✳ ✳ ✳

Remember Jesse Pujji? We met him back in chapter seven (Nod with Purpose) when he was building a Facebook-style platform for high schoolers. What exactly happened when he learned that Zuckerberg was working on the same project?

A few months into Pujji's venture, he realized he needed a website domain. Hsfacebook.com seemed like the perfect choice. But the domain owner had bad news for him: Zuckerberg was trying to buy the name too.

"We felt like we got punched in the gut," Pujji later described. Zuckerberg was *the* founder of Facebook. If what the domain owner said was true, Pujji didn't stand a chance. He had to see that it was real with his own eyes. So, he asked for proof.

The owner forwarded Pujji an email thread he had with Zuckerberg. At the bottom, it had Zuckerberg's phone number. Pujji didn't know it, but he had hit a door. He had the means to call one of the hottest founders at the time. He didn't wait to ask Zuckerberg if they could connect sometime—Pujji just picked up the phone and called.

The phone call lasted forty-five minutes. Zuckerberg spoke vehemently about Facebook. He outlined a clear vision of how people's Facebook accounts would become like a social ID, similar to a driver's license. In 2005, anyone would have called him crazy.

As Pujji followed Facebook's journey from the sidelines, he saw Zuckerberg's far-fetched vision manifest into the world. It showed him how powerful a founder's conviction can be in bringing a company to life. It's a lesson that has shaped his approach to entrepreneurship ever since. Looking back, he describes the call as one of the most transformative moments of his life.[163] Calling Zuckerberg was a door Pujji knocked on that swung open over a decade later when he decided to start his own company, and it was a door that required no permission.

This lack of permission is one of the key distinctions between doors and windows. While doors don't require permission, windows do. Medical school was the window Ali wanted to open. As a requirement for working in healthcare, medical school had a clear benefit. In order to open the window, he needed to ask for permission. He needed to do well on the BMAT.

Cambridge Medical School would become Ali's window. Soon, YouTube would be his door.

6med was teaching him a lot. As he built the company, he often felt the urge to write down the things he was learning. Starting a blog had always at the back of his mind.

The problem? "It all felt a bit narcissistic," Ali admitted to me. "I felt that people would think I'm arrogant to have the audacity to have a blog named after me. Who's got their own name as a domain if they're not super famous?"

But if he had learned one thing from 6med, it was the value of embracing uncertainty. That same year, Ali read a book about self-promotion as a creative called *Show Your Work*.[164] It made him feel slightly more comfortable with putting himself out there. A few months later, he bought the domain aliabdaal. com and started posting.

When I discovered Ali, I had already declared my hatred for StudyTube. It was a corner of the internet where students talked about productivity and posted videos on You-Tube with titles like "How Am I Always so Productive?" and "Fifteen-Hour Study with Me." As one magazine rebuked,

StudyTube embodied the idea that "to study successfully, studying must become one's personality, one's free time."[165]

On Ali's channel, I found those same studying and productivity tips. In one video, he talked about how he ranked first at Cambridge by memorizing thirty-five essays on every topic he thought his exams might include. He also posted hobby videos of his singing and medical analyses of Harry Potter. He cracked jokes about his love life and discussed his passion for keyboard shortcuts in great detail.

His view count, at the time, was subpar. "Did you have a plan for how to get more subscribers?" I asked him.

He shrugged. "Not really. I just kept posting."

His grit paid off. As of 2021, he has over 2 million subscribers on YouTube.

I've been watching his videos every week since. It's gotten me used to seeing his face in the sheen of good lighting with a tree and a bookshelf blurred artistically behind him.

Ali joined our video call from his phone, half-tilted behind another surface. "Sorry about the background noise," was the second thing he said to me. His parents were cooking in the next room. The man who had been giving me study tips since high school from three thousand miles away was, in fact, perfectly human.

As our interview began to wrap up, there was one question I had been wondering about ever since I first discovered his channel.

Entertainment star Tyler Perry advises people to "focus on one thing. Make it your priority and stick with it no matter what."[166] For Ali, medical school was not just a ploy to create clickbait content online—he is now both a full-time doctor and a full-time YouTuber. He also creates online courses, has his own podcast, and advises start-ups.

"Why do you stick with it all?" I asked him.

"With all of the stuff that I do, I aim for a reasonable standard instead of world-class," he said. "Life is just more fun when you're a jack of all trades."

World-class is relative—Ali makes over $1 million a year. Knocking eagerly on all kinds of doors made his success possible.

How can you find your own million-dollar doors to knock on?

SET FEAR

What's the worst that could happen? It's a question every fictional character has asked themselves right before they find out exactly how bad things can get.

Luckily, the real world is less hungry for irony than the fictional world. According to Tim Ferris, reflecting on the worst that can happen is a pretty good use of your time.

When you knock on the door of an opportunity, you have no idea what you'll find on the other side. That lack of certainty breeds fear.

What if a scary monster opens the door?

What if no one opens it and you're stuck knocking outside forever?

But what if the stuff of your wildest dreams was waiting on the other side?

When conquering uncertain decisions, Ferriss believes in weighing these questions. He calls it "fear-setting." It's an activity he discovered when he was overworked and felt like his company was about to shatter any second. He was insecure, cranky, and pessimistic about the future.

It was at this time the idea of a sabbatical crossed his mind. He wanted a pause button on his work-crazed life. A trip around the world offered just that. Ferriss agonized over the idea for months. What's the worst that could happen?

"My business could fail while I'm overseas, for sure," he thought in response. "A legal warning letter would accidentally not get forwarded and I would get sued."

The situation escalated uncontrollably in his mind. It ended with someone spitting on his head from a high-rise balcony while he was feeding food scraps to a stray dog. Naturally, the dog would get nervous from the saliva and bite him in the face.[167]

To conquer fear, you have to define it. When you define it, you realize how ridiculous it is.

Fear-setting involves writing out the worst possible situation that could result from your decision. How permanent would it be? How likely is it? What steps could you take if it happened? Then, you write down the best possible situation that could ensue. How possible is it? How life-changing would it be? Writing your thoughts down forces you to reconcile them.

For most doors, the worst possible situation is nothing happening at all. No one watches your videos. No one signs up for your class. No one pays attention when you speak up at a meeting. And the best possible situation? Some combination of innovation, empowerment, and happiness.

For Ferris, the worst possible consequence of his sabbatical was his business going under. If it did, he realized he could just take up a job as a bartender until he found another stream of income. The best possible consequence was enlightenment on better ways to live his life.

"There was practically no risk," he reflected. "Only huge life-changing upside potential."[168]

Fear-setting helps us accept the uncertainty of knocking on doors. Why does leaning into ambiguity still seem so hard?

BALANCE DOORS WITH WINDOWS

The problem is people crave instant gratification.

David Laibson, a professor at Harvard University, describes the issue as a conflict between our "emotional brain" and our "logical brain." Your emotional brain has "a hard time imagining the future, even though your logical brain clearly sees the future consequences of your current actions."[169] Your logical brain knows the consequence of distraction is not being able to finish your work, but your emotional brain craves the dopamine influx of reading a notification.

Deadlines create short-term gratification. Meeting a deadline gives your brain a feeling of fulfillment—you completed something successfully. It's why, no matter how long you procrastinate, you usually get your work done in the end.

The human brain craves this predictability. It's not just deadlines—results can also foster the feeling. If you study for that calculus exam for twelve hours, you will get an A. If you fine-tune your resumé and do practice interviews, you will get a job.

With door-knocking, you have no way to envision the future consequences of your actions. In high school, Ali didn't know that not learning to code would be the difference between zero and 1 million YouTube subscribers.

Why'd he do it?

Part of Ali's comfort with knocking on so many doors was that he also opened windows. Pursuing medicine was one of those windows. While the journey through medical school was grueling, he got a respectable, stable job in return. Having that stability allowed him to knock on many doors, even if they proved unfruitful. For the underdog who cannot afford to lose, balancing your doors with windows is especially crucial.

Windows don't have to be six-years-of-medical-school-intense in order to soften the blow of a door slamming in your face. They could be pitching your product to your close friends and family, so you have their support when you launch to the public. They could be devoting extra time to your hiring process so you recruit the most talented people for your team. What extra cushioning would make you feel more comfortable with taking a risk? Spend your energy trying to budge that window open.[170]

* * *

"Never give a mouse a cookie," I told my mom, beaming, when she asked me what I learned in school that day.

I was eight years old and had just read a book called *If You Give a Mouse a Cookie*. "If you give a mouse a cookie," it starts, "he's going to ask for a glass of milk."

To drink the milk, the mouse needs a straw. When he finishes slurping the milk down, he'll need to check the mirror (as one does) to make sure he doesn't have a milk mustache. During the story, the mouse trims his hair, sweeps the bathroom floor, cleans the house, reads a story, draws a picture, and hangs it on your refrigerator.

When he sees the refrigerator, he is reminded he is thirsty. He'll ask you for a glass of milk. And what could go better with that than a cookie?[171]

The story is reminiscent of the Butterfly Effect, the idea that small things can have colossal effects on the world.[172] A butterfly flapping its wings might cause a tornado. A little boy learning to code might make him a millionaire. Giving a mouse a cookie might just cost you two.

Knocking on doors is a leap of faith. While most doors don't have any effect on your life at all, one door could drastically shift your entire trajectory. When you consistently pursue opportunities that have no obvious reward, you maximize your chances of one of them colossally changing your life.

So, knock. Knock like you're a dad who doesn't believe in texting. Knock like you're a kid who doesn't want to lose their second cookie. Knock like you can barely wait to get inside. Keep knocking until you do.

What's the worst that could happen?

KNOCK ON THE DOOR

- Knock on doors by seeking experiences relatively low-effort but offering no clear reward. This is how you will find many of the best opportunities.

- To balance the risk of this uncertainty, open windows, which require a bit of extra work but offer a clear reward.

- Ask for permission sparingly when knocking on doors. You can always seek forgiveness later.

- When you're feeling uncertain about pursuing an opportunity, try fear-setting. Write down what the worst possible outcome could be. Consider how likely it is and how you could deal with it if it happened. Then, write down the best possible outcome. Weigh both scenarios and then decide.

CHAPTER 11

DEFY THE PINCERS

———

When you can, lean into hardship. Your unique experiences
with a problem equip you to be the best potential solver of it.

–ALEXANDRIA LAFCI

Strawberry ice cream dripped down my fingers. My dad eyed
the scoops now losing their form nervously.

But my attention was far from the pink staining my hands.
I was enraptured with the claw machine. It was such a good
deal—drop in two quarters and you could leave the carnival
like a princess, clutching a larger-than-life stuffed unicorn.

I always loved carnivals as a child. It was something about the
smell of fresh funnel cake and the shrieks of excited children;
the sticky fingers and the spinning around in a teacup until
the world looked like the inside of a kaleidoscope.

"Kid, I think your ice..."

Splat.

Surprisingly, my tragic flaw at carnivals was never the ice
cream that would inevitably drop from the cone—it was the

claw machine. I would watch other kids walk away with their stuffed dinosaurs and puppies and giraffes, but the unicorn I had my eye on remained watching me from behind the glass.

I didn't know it then, but my detailed algebraic calculations of where to position the claw for the perfect grasp were in vain. Claw machines are rigged. They are programmed to have a strong grip only a fraction of the time. Often, this is set manually by the owner based on desired profit.[173]

For example, if the owners want a profit of about 50 percent, they might set their machine so it operates on full power once every twenty-three tries. As the player, you have no way of knowing in advance how often the machine is designed to work. If you really want the prize, you have to keep dropping quarters until the machine regains its strength.

Life for underdogs works in a similar way. It's often rigged against us, but we can brute-force our way through. While it can feel like our repeated attempts are in vain, we never know when the pincers will manage to hold on. If you're at a point where you feel like things just aren't working, you might just be on try number twenty-two.

How do you know if the game is rigged or just plain broken? I went to entrepreneur Alexandria Lafci for answers.

* * *

Alexandria still remembers the first time she felt disappointed in adults.

She was a little girl on a road trip in Turkey, where her family on her dad's side lived. They pulled over to fill up the car with gas. A child around her age was standing there, holding a sign. She was wide-eyed and begging for food.

It was clear to Alexandria that the girl was hungry, but her family shooed her off and quickly drove away. It was then Alexandria decided she had to be different as a grown-up: "If I'm able to be helpful in a situation to a fellow human being, I must be."

I met Alexandria on a Wednesday morning. She was bundled up in a shawl and her voice was low. As she described the injustices she had watched growing up, her posture straightened.

"I lived in Section 8 [government-assisted] housing and was surrounded by low-income communities," she said. "There were definitely times when the heat was shut down or the lights were off." She was raised by a single black mother who also grew up in the foster care system and wanted to create a better life for her daughter.

Many of Alexandria's close friends and family were living on food stamps and minimum wage. "Then I would go into private schools or be on an honors track at school, and I saw a very different lifestyle," she said. "That juxtaposition was stark."

When she was fifteen, Alexandria stumbled upon a program that allowed high schoolers to go on a trip to Peru and volunteer. She went to her mother with bright eyes and hope.

"You can go if you can fund it," her mother said. It was a soft no.

For Alexandria, it was a green light. All she had to do was find the money. Where could she look?

* * *

Tim Ferriss had to bribe his students.

The entrepreneur was scanning an eager crowd of undergraduates, hands raised and brimming with questions, during his guest lecture at Princeton University on entrepreneurship. The problem? "Most students would go out and promptly do the opposite of what I preached," Ferriss wrote on his blog. They "would be putting in 80-hour weeks as high-paid coffee fetchers unless I showed that the principles from class could actually be applied."

He decided to offer them a challenge: contact three people who seem impossible to reach (think Bill Gates or Taylor Swift) and get one of them to respond to three questions of the student's choosing. Ferriss would buy a round-trip ticket anywhere in the world for whoever did the best job.

Twenty students were present. It was a self-selecting group: the original class was around sixty students. These twenty students were the ones who had expressed interest in his challenge. They were "frothing at the mouth to win a free spin across the globe," Ferriss recalled.

Zero of them ultimately tried.[174]

The challenge was hard. None of the students wanted to be outdone. If anyone had taken a shot, they would have won by default, even if their email was a sentence written by a pre-schooler and their celebrities never responded.

Because everyone was apprehensive about the competition, the competition never commenced.

We shy from opportunities when we think our likelihood of success is low. This is especially true for underdogs. Women, for example, are 26 percent less likely to ask for a job referral than men. On average, they also tend to apply to jobs only when they meet 100 percent of the requirements, while men apply when they meet 60 percent.[175] When things feel out of reach, underdogs eliminate themselves before the race even begins.

While doing hard things is hard, doing the impossible is a little easier.

NUMBER OF PEOPLE
WILLING TO DO
HARD THINGS

NUMBER OF PEOPLE
WILLING TO DO
THE IMPOSSIBLE

For Alexandria, the question was not *where* to look, but rather, if she was *willing* to look. She lived in a low-income neighborhood, but about a mile away from her home, people lived in a wealthy area with big, beautiful homes. The solution was simple. "I wrote a bunch of handwritten letters, I walked over to that nice neighborhood, and I just dropped them in their mailboxes."

Most people would be intimidated by the prospect of asking for help from a stranger, so Alexandria's letter was probably the only one like that in those families' mailboxes. Trying isn't half the battle. It *is* the battle.

About a month and a half later, someone agreed to fund Alexandria's trip to Peru. She was elated.

But in the grand scheme of things, does some random high school trip really matter?

* * *

In recent years, there has been a lot of backlash against service trips from wealthy countries to developing ones. One paper from the University of Colorado Denver suggests these trips may do more harm than good, as volunteers come in with little understanding of the local infrastructure.[176] Another paper argues these trips reinforce paternalism: the country receiving the service is expected to be passively grateful, regardless of whether the volunteers' work has a positive impact.[177]

Alexandria loved her time in Peru—but as she was leaving, she felt subdued. Unless there was another plane full of people like her who were coming in the opposite direction, there would be no one to sustain the schools and orphanages she had spent hours engaging with.

"We had created this system where these clinics, these schools, these orphanages had become dependent on volunteers," she told me. There *had* to be a better way.

Alexandria didn't know it then, but the approach she was looking for was sustainable development. She wanted a system to help people that could become self-sustaining over time.

In college, Alexandria studied international relations.[178]

One of the experiences she remembers most vividly is her time interning at the African Presidential Center at Boston University. Every year, they brought together current and former African presidents to discuss important topics about the future of their continent.

"I was writing briefs that presidents and their teams were going to read," she recalled. "I was speaking with leaders of nations at such an early age. Those experiences gave me confidence." Alexandria felt ready to change the world.

But a few years after college, she was wielding gloves and stapling papers. She was working at an industrial and commercial supplier in Atlanta. She was miserable. What had happened?

✳ ✳ ✳

We live in a world relative to the people around us. If you call Kevin Durant tall, what you really mean is, "Kevin Durant is 6'10" and most men are about 5'9". Therefore, he is tall."

Comparison is inherent to the way we see the world. Most times, this is completely harmless. In fact, it makes things easier for our brain to process. *Russia is large. Apples are sweet. This book is good.* These kinds of statements are easy to make because we have a pool of information with which to compare. We compare countries with other countries and fruits with other fruits. Imagine how difficult it would be to judge someone's height if we had never seen another person before. It would be cognitively taxing, if not, impossible.[179]

The problem arises when we begin comparing achievements. *He's twenty-one years old and a millionaire, but I'm fifty-three and still struggling to pay rent. She has perfect grades, but I have straight Bs.* According to social psychologist Leon Festinger's social comparison theory, these kinds of judgments influence how we determine our worth.[180]

In a life often like a claw machine, they are misplaced.

During her time working in Atlanta, Alexandria attended a social entrepreneurship conference. There, she met Matthew Marshall, a user experience design consultant, and Brett Hagler, a growth director. It was 2014, four years after a 7.0 magnitude earthquake rocked Haiti.

Hagler had recently gone on a volunteer trip to the country. He was shocked by what he saw. While people around the world had raised billions of dollars in relief funds for the country, tens of thousands of Haitian people still had no home. As of 2015, the Red Cross had reportedly built just six permanent structures for the earthquake survivors.[181]

The culprits? Poor administration and a lack of transparency.

Alexandria knew firsthand how horrible housing insecurity was, and she wanted to help. She joined forces with Hagler and Marshall to help accelerate housing developments in Haiti. They called their nonprofit New Story Charity. They hoped their work would be the start of a "new story" for the people they built homes for.

From that moment, things began to pick up quickly. Within a year, the team was accepted into YC as one of the accelerator's first charities ever.[182] In that time span, they also built sixty-two homes.

It was more than ten times what the Red Cross had built in Haiti…in 20 percent of the time.

In a space where a few organizations had been dominating the space for years, Alexandria and the New Story team beat all industry norms. They successfully won a rigged game.

How can you do the same?

DROP A PENNY

The great thing about claw machines is they are very accepting of all the random coins littering the bottom of your bag: the quarters, the pennies, and everything in between.

With so many organizations out in the world building homes, it's hard to understand why New Story was so successful. In fact, the initiative started out as a mere crowdfunding platform that raised money to build homes. Innovation and novelty were far from the team's minds—they were trying to help in any small way they could. Over time, as they grew more adept at growing the nonprofit, they began dropping more coins into their idea.

Expanding to El Salvador. *Clink.*

Partnering with Salesforce and Goldman Sachs. *Clink.*

Investing in technology research. *Clink.*

Developing a 3D printer. *Clink clink.*

Building a community of 3D-printed homes. *Clink clink clink.*

It was the first community of its kind. The team printed an entire home in less than a day for $4,000. The average cost of constructing a home at the time was $289,415.[183]

While traditional housing charities were building wooden, shack-style homes that collapsed at a whisper of the wind, Alexandria insisted on the homes being well-designed.

"Very often we as a society are willing to accept 'less than' for this type of population: 'less than' in quality, 'less than' for innovation, 'less than' great design," she said in a 2019 interview with *Fast Company*. "Even when populations are seemingly vulnerable, or seemingly will accept whatever is given, that's not an excuse to not push to have the highest quality of whoever you're working with."[184]

Each New Story house is built with a printer that squeezes out liquid concrete in layers. The inside is decorated with lighting and architectural details to make the space feel like home. Fun geometric details give each house its own unique character.

Despite being a nonprofit, much of New Story's infrastructure today is reminiscent of a start-up. The organization is consistently deemed one of the most innovative nonprofits in the world and ranks highly among architectural corporations for its strides in design.[185]

And so, the claw machine spurred to life.

In a world huge and brimming with cool projects, coming up with something brand new is intimidating. Waiting, then, becomes one of the biggest traps in innovation. Intuition tells us to wait until our idea is perfect, but as LinkedIn cofounder Reid Hoffman says, "If you're not embarrassed by the first version of your product, you've launched too late."

Home rental platform Airbnb began as a few airbeds the founders rented out to strangers on the internet.[186] Work communication tool Slack began as a role-playing video game.[187] Both companies are now billion-dollar corporations.

No one starts a venture knowing exactly what they are doing. Underdogs often have even less certainty. But everyone has a penny to spare. Dropping it into your claw machine gives you a place to start. Do it. Do it better. Then do it right.

1 DAY

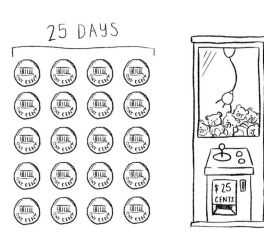

25 DAYS

Pennies are a great place to start because they're so accessible. After hearing *clink* after *clink* of pennies hitting the bottom of your machine, at some point you'll want the boost of a shiny dime. Where do you look?

MEET THEM WHERE THEY MINGLE

There used to be a coffee shop in San Francisco known as The Creamery. It looked like someone had carved a modern coffee shop out of an antique dairy with wooden beams encompassing an airy interior.

It was the kind of coffee shop where you'd hear the soft clatter of venture capitalists typing on their laptops and the eager voices of scruffy hipsters asking you to beta test their app. On any given day, listening in on conversations inside would give you a crash course on what was happening in the world of Silicon Valley.

People didn't go to The Creamery for its subpar coffee or free Wi-Fi. They went to The Creamery to fraternize with Silicon Valley's elite.

When founder Ryan Mickle was trying to raise funds for his start-up, he repeatedly emailed his dream investor with no response. One day, Mickle learned the investor stopped in at The Creamery on weekends. So, he amended his email. Instead of sending the investor his pitch deck for the dozenth time, Mickle asked if he could stop by for coffee on Sunday. He got his response within ten minutes: "Sure, come on down."[188]

While you may have only pennies to drop into your claw machine, other people can give you dimes. When you're the underdog, these people don't come to you. Instead, you have to meet them where they mingle. For small Bay Area founders in the 2010s hoping to secure big checks, that place was The Creamery.

Know anyone you wish would lend you a dime?

For Airbnb founders Brian Chesky, Nathan Blecharczyk, and Joe Gebbia, their wish was wealthy New York homeowners. They met them where they were—at the front doors of their homes. "We literally would knock on the doors of all of our hosts," Chesky recalls. "We'd say, 'Hey, this is Brian, Joe, we're founders and we just want to meet you.'"

In exchange for the homeowner's time, Chesky and his cofounders would photograph the person's home and help them upload it onto their website. Many of them were hesitant about using the platform, but because the founders were right at their door, they could address it immediately.

If the homeowner said, "Hey, I don't feel comfortable with the guest. I don't know who they are," Chesky would ask, "Well, what if we had profiles?" The homeowner's eyes would light up. This is how the team created new product features and got their first homes listed for rent on the platform.[189]

When you're the underdog, you often only have pennies, but there are many people out there who have nickels, dimes, and quarters. Figure out who those people are for you. Where do they reside? What areas do they circulate? Where are they most comfortable? Don't wait for people to discover you—seek people where they are.

* * *

As of today, New Story has built over 2,700 homes. Alexandria is still in awe of their work. "Watching families move into their homes—that's the best part of the job," she tells me, smiling. "When families see their home for the first time they touch the walls. They feel like, 'This is safe. I can close my door. I can lock it. This is the room where my kids can sleep.'"

When I told my father about Alexandria's story, he shook his head. "Seeing what she is building makes me feel like I am doing nothing with my life."

His words echoed how I felt when I was that little kid in a carnival, staring with longing at other kids' stuffed animals and wondering why I couldn't win what they had won. When we begin thinking about how our achievements stack up against someone else's, our perception of our own worth diminishes.

The reality of being the underdog is we often encounter claw machines that need twenty-three quarters before they return to full strength. Others may encounter the machine when it only needs one more quarter. Comparing our own success to theirs is fruitless.

Alexandria had been dropping quarters into the same claw machine since she was fifteen. Her high school service trip helped her uncover her passion and her corporate job in Atlanta taught her the organizational skills necessary to be a chief operating officer.

Alexandria successfully won a rigged game by defying the pincers. All you need is a few pennies to do the same.

DEFY THE PINCERS

- Life is like a claw machine. While it takes everyone the same amount of coins to be successful, each person starts with a different number of coins in their machine. Comparing yourself to others is fruitless.

- When you're taking on a big project, start by taking small steps instead of waiting until you can afford to take a big one.

- Make a list of people who could exponentially help you with your projects. Then, find out where they naturally circulate, whether it's a physical place or an online platform. Seek them out in these places.

CHAPTER 12

THE ART OF NAIVETY

———

Hope is what keeps me going. I am an optimist of the first order.

—ALICE WATERS

If you've never been to a fancy cooking event in New York, that makes two of us. I'd imagine dimmed lights, though, with food sculptures named after fancy European-sounding delicacies I've never heard of, forks and knives made of gold, and many middle-aged men with trimmed beards crossing their arms and admiring their work smugly.

If you happened to be at one particular culinary event sometime in the 1970s, you'd find I was mostly right. In the midst of it all, you'd find a woman looking slightly flustered, clutching a bowl with a mere garden salad in it. Alice Waters was profusely apologizing to anyone who cared to give her a second glance that day.

Among the delicacies journalists had to pretend they could pronounce, her salad was an outlier. They didn't know that she'd picked the vegetables fresh from the ground of her own garden just days before the event. She'd made the dressing in a bowl she'd borrowed from legendary chef James Beard. Then she'd excitedly carried it with her all the way to New York.

"It's James Beard's salad bowl," she tried to explain as people observed her salad with raised eyebrows. She was embarrassed.

But the next day, it was her plain old salad the *New York Times* was talking about. Sometimes, it pays to be naive. But what was it about that salad?

* * *

If you walk through a grocery store today, your eyes are likely to be bombarded with flashy labels touting their organic, farm-fresh produce. These products often cost twice as much as their non-organic counterparts and shoppers are more than happy to pay the premium. There is no question about it: organic *sells*.[190]

Things were not always this way. In the 1940s and 1950s, the editor of an international magazine dreamed of a world where his work would emancipate women from sandwich-making forever.

His magazine? *Quick Frozen Foods.* It was a news publication that reported on the international frozen foods market. At the time, this market was the fastest-growing sector in the food industry. Frozen foods were depicted as a convenient, affordable holy grail that would pave the way for a progressive economy.[191]

Alice grew up in this world of processed food. It was during World War II. Her parents had to feed four children, including herself. Many days they were struggling to put food on the table. When they did have food, it was meat, potatoes, and a fruit cup—food from a can or frozen. "I didn't like food very much," she mused to me.

Despite being a self-declared picky eater, a few years later, Alice found herself in Paris, standing eagerly in line for hot baguettes. When her baguettes finally came, she slathered on fresh strawberry jam and scarfed them down eagerly with her friends. *Surely, there was something otherworldly in this jam,* she thought.

Alice peeked her head into the kitchen, hoping to catch a glimpse of the chef's secrets. When she asked where the strawberries in the jam came from, they shot her a glance. "Well, you just have to go out into the woods and pick them." Alice wasn't a picky eater—she had just never eaten fresh food before.

Upon realizing this, she began watching the French wide-eyed as they went about their bustling local markets. No one called them farmer's markets—didn't every market have food from farmers? Watching French people live so ordinarily while having a seemingly radical diet made Alice feel accessible fresh produce wasn't so radical after all.

Eating food in America didn't feel the same when she came back home.

She was a college student at UC Berkeley. It was the 1960s, a time when the Free Speech movement had taken hold of the school. Between classes and distant dreams of French food, Alice watched her fellow students protest. Coming from a secluded, suburban town, she had never thought about politics so deeply.

Intrigued, Alice would listen to Mario Savio, a student leader of the movement. He spoke to crowds about fighting back against injustice, eyebrows furrowed and head furiously nodding: "There's a time when the operation of the machine becomes so odious, makes you so sick at heart, that you can't take part! [...] And you've got to put your bodies upon the gears and upon the wheels, [...] upon all the apparatus, and you've got to make it stop!"[192]

Savio spoke of changing the world. Listening to him, Alice felt inspired to change it too. The question that remained: how?

* * *

I still remember the first time I made ravioli. My friend (a more gifted cook than I was) grinned when I told her I hadn't salted the water before boiling the pasta. "Amateur," she scoffed.

I barely heard her. I was too awestruck at what I had created.

The word *amateur* comes from the Old French term *ameour,* which means "lover." While the essence of the word has been distorted by negative connotations of poor performance, the word amateur is about love. Amateurs do what they do for love. Professionals do it for money.

When Radiohead frontman Thom Yorke was asked what his greatest strength was, he nonchalantly replied, "That I don't know what I'm doing." Whenever he felt like his songwriting was growing stale, he would pick up an instrument he had never played and try to write a song with it.[193] It took him back to being an amateur—free from the bonds of money and quality, he could focus on loving his craft.

Alice fell in love with food before she cared about how it was made.

When she couldn't find authentic French food in Berkeley, she tried to make her own. Through daily practice, her food became edible enough to feed to others. Her friends would gather around her table to talk about the revolution every night as she stumbled her way through cooking them pâté en croûte.

"It was radical chic," her former roommate Eleanor Bertino later described. "All these people would come through their modest little bungalow, Alice would cook this lovely dinner, then more people would come."[194]

Feeding so many people fresh food every night was not sustainable. While nothing could top the whopping $30,000 of annual culinary school tuition, Alice was still going broke learning how to cook. How could she practice cooking for her friends while still making income?

* * *

Few people set out to be entrepreneurs the way they became a doctor or an engineer. Yet, in many schools and universities, entrepreneurship is taught the same way as science: through textbooks and multiple-choice exams.

Economist and entrepreneur Carl Schramm is one outspoken advocate against this approach. He says in order to foster innovation, entrepreneurs need to "burn the business plan."[195] Businesses are not like cooking—a few cups of responsible financial planning with a sprinkle of digital marketing do not make a successful business. Writing a business plan the way you would write a cookbook is pointless.

Empirical evidence is on Schramm's side. Of entrepreneurs who have had a successful exit (i.e., either sold their company or had an IPO), 70 percent did not start with a business plan.[196]

There is still a line between no business plan and making wholly irresponsible business decisions.

Alice was teetering on the edge.

As she pondered how to pay for all the groceries lining her fridge, she couldn't stop thinking about one idea in particular: opening her own restaurant. It made sense logically. Given her love for food, a restaurant could be the best source of income for her.

While Alice had no money of her own to pay for a restaurant, her parents and a few of her "counterculture" friends were willing to lend her some. Who could she turn to for the rest of the money she needed? Well, it was the 1970s, and word on the street had it that one group of people was making quite a big sum of cash off hippies on the street.

Alice was finally able to buy a place in 1971 with money she had borrowed from Berkeley's local drug dealers.

The "place" was an old plumbing shop inside a house in North Berkeley. The awe in Alice's voice was palpable as she described the house, with its exposed pipes and small, overgrown court-yard in the front. To have a restaurant inside a home was perfect. "It would feel like I'm cooking at home."

Others were less kind. It was "an ugly, squat, two-story, Hol-lywood-type stucco apartment house that I tore apart with four or five hippie carpenters," described Paul Aratow, an early supporter and film director. Still, Aratow and a few others hammered away at the home. They furnished it with miscel-laneous objects from the local flea market and posters they had painted themselves. They called it Chez Panisse.

The run-down home that became one of the most famous restaurants in the United States.

On the first night, Alice served pâté en croûte, duck with olives, potatoes with celery root puree, and a pastry. She charged just $3.95 for the entire meal. Her friends bustled around the kitchen as Alice greeted customers at the door.

Chez Panisse grew up in this world of friends helping friends keep their labor of love afloat. The initial plan was for the restaurant to serve breakfast, lunch, and dinner, seven days a week, from seven a.m. to two a.m. While they quickly found these hours unrealistic, the spirit of intensely hard work never left the restaurant.[197]

Alice had specific desires for every aspect of the place, from how cheap the food was to be (she wanted Chez Panisse to be accessible) to which kinds of farmers from which they would source each vegetable. The menu changed every day so her employees could innovate and the food was made with the freshest produce available on that particular day. Her friends trudged along.

But with so many people's livelihoods depending on the restaurant, goodwill did not seem like it could compensate for a lack of business intuition. Even as the restaurant gained rapid popularity among locals, money in the bank was dwindling. Suppliers were irritated with the irregular payments. Employees needed to feed their families.

"We really needed help," Alice admitted to me. Anyone know a place with lifelines for $3.95?

* * *

When I met Alice, it was hard for me to reconcile the portrait of a woman who was desperate to merely keep her restaurant afloat with the local Berkeley celebrity in front of me. She spoke with shining eyes and a lilt about her deep-seated belief in accessible, fresh food—even as the restaurant she had worked so hard to build was falling apart around her. When I asked what her strategy for keeping Chez Panisse alive was at the time, she shrugged, laughing lightly. "If you burned the corn soup, you called it grilled corn soup."

To a restaurant veteran, her response would exude naivety, but it reminded me of one of my mother's favorite principles from the Montessori method of teaching.

When she teaches her students about colors, she doesn't tell them red and blue make purple. Instead, she lets them mix different pigmented dyes and write down what they observe. They fumble with the dyes and discover that while mixing red and green dye creates a mundane gray-brown color, combining red and blue dye creates an absolutely royal purple. Her students don't learn by listening—they learn by doing.

As Alice fumbled with the ropes of entrepreneurship, she was employing a process that would make my mother proud. Because she had no prior experience as a restaurateur, she did things and then leaned on iteration and improvisation to figure out what worked and what didn't.

When her friend who collected fresh mussels for the restaurant showed her the dumpster in the back, telling her to get in and *smell* the effects of her carelessness with trash, she learned about reducing the waste she generated. When she found that demand for the restaurant was outstripping supply, she learned about operations management and how to effectively expand capacity. When she began to lose money, she learned how to incorporate as a corporation and gave away shares of the restaurant. When she lost her first employee, she learned how to retain the rest.

In 1973, James Beard stumbled upon Chez Panisse on a visit to the Bay Area. He declared it one of the four best restaurants in the United States. Beard, known as "The Dean of American Cuisine," was one of the most famous food critics in America at the time.

Suddenly, Chez Panisse was no longer a surprise find for tourists who happened to be in Berkeley. Berkeley became the find for tourists flying over just to try the lauded restaurant. Chez Panisse, and by extension its fight against fast-food culture, exploded.

Alice didn't embrace being the underdog—she never knew she was one in the first place. Her naivety bred the innovation that led Chez Panisse to become a national phenomenon. How can you do the same?

THE TRANSLUCENT TUNNEL METHOD

We live in a time of information overload. We can access almost any data we want, when and where we want it. Social worker and educator Libby Simon describes the experience: "I know the world is turning on its axis, but somebody must be stepping on the accelerator pedal because my head is spinning."[198]

If you've ever watched CNN, you'll know exactly what she's talking about: rapidly changing panels of reporters talking from around the world with flashing headlines moving across the bottom of the screen. It's a microcosm of the world we live in: rapid, loud, and packed with information.

The consequences of information overload are tangible. One study by Hewlett-Packard found the IQ scores of knowledge workers fell by an average of ten points when they were distracted by notifications and stray pieces of information.

That's double the mental decline noted from smoking medical marijuana.[199]

We criticize people who we perceive to have "tunnel vision"—people who focus incessantly on one thing while ignoring the rest. With so much information around us, what makes hyperfocus a bad thing? For Alice, tunnel vision allowed her to plow through failure. Her eyes were focused on the light at the end: farm-fresh food for all.

While people may say that if you have tunnel vision, you will be oblivious to important things happening in the world, not all tunnels are opaque. Some are translucent.

When you live your life in a translucent tunnel, you can see what is around you, but your vision is limited by what actually matters. You have the power to choose what to care about and what to ignore.

As neuroscientist Dr. Wendy Suzuki explains, that control could not be more important for innovation. Many of the morsels of information you're exposed to can make you fearful, anxious, and reluctant. You may think, "is there truly a point in applying to that program when its acceptance rate is 2 percent?"

Over a long period of time, fear shrinks the size of your hippocampus, a part of your brain that's critical for long-term memory. Because imagination requires taking things from your memory and putting them together in new ways, fear hinders your imagination. It is literally "zapping your creativity."[200]

On the other hand, when you live life in a tunnel, you have less to be fear. Your tunnel gives your mind the space to find unexpected links in your memories. It gives your mind the freedom to innovate.

It's a tunnel you build as you go. You choose what goes in it and what stays outside as life takes its twists and turns. Unexplored territories can fall within the scope of the tunnel, but other things must be excluded in their place. The tunnel's width is limited, as is your capacity for information.

How do you determine how to build your tunnel? Where is ignorance not only blissful but also conducive to innovation?

IT'S AN ART, NOT A SCIENCE

For Alice, one of the things inside her tunnel was the Montessori method of education, the same method my mother looks to when she preaches learning by doing.

Alice did Montessori training in England before opening her restaurant. "It showed me how our senses can create pathways to our minds," she told me, eyes shining.

Montessori was about helping children fall in love with learning, but Alice used it to help people fall in love with her food. Every part of Chez Panisse was designed to light up people's senses: fragrant rosemary, a crackling fire, and a warm-toned open kitchen.

Alice stayed focused on the two things she loved most—Montessori and fresh produce. Most other things, like prestige and recognition, stayed in the terrain outside her tunnel.

Montessori and food is not a combination that intuitively makes sense, which is exactly what makes this entire process an art. Tunnel-building is about bringing in all of the ideas you love to think about. Then, cut out the information you consume only because you feel like you need to know it—whether it's the acceptance rate of that program you're applying to or the empty criticism your work is getting on social media.

The benefit for Alice was measurable. Her lack of awareness about the cooking world allowed her to be bold and do the things she loved unabashedly. "I was so naive, but that made it simple," she explained.

Even when I talked to Alice, she seemed to carry that same naivety with her. She didn't know her restaurant had been deemed one of the most influential of its time by *TIME* magazine. She shrugged laughingly when I asked her about the challenges of being in a space so heavily male-dominated. But her eyes lit up when I told her my mother was a Montessori-trained teacher.

For Maria Montessori, the founder of the Montessori teaching philosophy, her tunnel brought together medicine and children. Growing up in the late nineteenth century, Montessori learned very early on she would have to actively exclude societal norms from her tunnel if she wanted to act on her ambitions.

While those around her exclaimed that women couldn't possibly pursue medicine, Montessori studied diligently for university entrance exams and appealed her case to the pope. Eventually, she became the first female doctor in Italy.

The people in her middle-class circles found her strange, and it wasn't just because she was a woman who loved science. When she came out of school, she spent much of her time with children who had developmental disabilities and lived in Italian slums. Her neighbors wrinkled their noses at her, whispering that there was something *odd* and *animal-like* about children like *that*.

But Montessori's intuition of medicine could not reconcile this: how could there be something inhumane about human beings? She spent hours working with the children, helping them make sense of the complicated, often hostile world around them. Soon, they were passing "normal children" exams with flying colors.[201]

The theories Montessori formulated during this time provided the foundation for her namesake method of teaching, a method considered as innovative as it was radical. In her creation process, society's estrangement of her proved to be a gift. It helped her build her tunnel with their ideas well out of sight. It helped her focus on the work she loved most.

"Sense" and "nonsense" are products of the status quo. They represent the natural order of things currently, rather than what that natural order could be in the future. In the race for innovation, the status quo is your biggest enemy—to innovate is to actively work against it.

Translucent tunnels help you innovate by giving you a barrier between yourself and the status quo. So, lean into nonsense and the things that intuitively seem like they wouldn't fit as you build your tunnel. The more divergent the things inside are, the better. Building is an art, not a science.

* * *

In Berkeley, public school children learn about math, science, reading, and writing while working in kitchen and garden classrooms. They sow seeds, pull weeds, dice vegetables, and they always set the table.[202]

When investors saw the phenomenon Chez Panisse was becoming, their million-dollar checks were practically jumping out of their pockets. They imagined hundreds of Chez Panisse restaurants, signed Alice Waters posters, and branded packaged foods on grocery store shelves everywhere.

Alice had other plans.

She believed healthy food should be a right, not a privilege. She wanted to start a movement. She called it The Edible Schoolyard Project. Her goal was to help children learn about food and gain access to healthy produce.

She began her work at Martin Luther King Jr. Middle School in Berkeley, CA. Today, the Edible Schoolyard Networks connects more than 5,800 kitchen and garden education programs from 53 US states and territories as well as 75 countries around the world. Alice is credited with pioneering the farm-to-table movement and inspiring Michelle Obama's organic vegetable garden in the White House.[203]

Alice's story highlights that a little bit of naivety can go a long (start-a-global-movement-long) way. So, what does your tunnel look like? Does it ever overwhelm you with information? Does it scare you away or does it excite you? And, optionally, does it make your mouth water for some fresh salad?

THE ART OF NAIVETY

- Embrace naivety and the freedom that comes with it. When you let go of the anxiety of expertise, you can think more deeply and creatively.

- Move through life like you're inside a translucent tunnel. Surround yourself with ideas that inspire you and actively avoid information that discourages you.

- The best way to learn is by doing. Instead of trying to cram how-tos, start that project you've been thinking about and then iterate.

- Don't be afraid to combine ideas that seem like they don't belong together. Innovation is about challenging the status quo's norms.

CHAPTER 13

ENJOY THE RIDE

———

Fun is not about finding the treasure. It's about defeating the puzzle.

—HARPER REED

"You have to be a total lunatic to start a company," Michael Seibel said.

He was scanning a screen of students who drooled over start-ups. We were taking a class on entrepreneurship and Seibel was the guest lecturer that day. We watched wide-eyed as he scoffed at us. "Start-ups have a 99.9 percent failure rate. Why would anyone want to do that to themselves?"

Seibel was the CEO of YC and cofounder of Twitch, a company he sold to Amazon for almost $1 billion.[204] He was one of the start-up world's most sought-after advisors.

"Go become a doctor or a banker," Seibel advised with a grin. "The success rate is higher and you'll probably make more money." We stared back dazedly.

A week later, I got on a video call to interview Harper Reed, an entrepreneur and one of Silicon Valley's go-to technologists.

He had thick black glasses, a scraggly beard, and a silver earring peeking out from behind his facial hair. His virtual background looked like a TV breaking news frame. The headline flashed, "Too many bananas? Is that a thing?" in big capital letters. His head looked like it was floating in outer space.

"Hi, Harper!" I chirped. "How are you doing?"

"I had too many bananas," he replied blankly.

Michael Seibel was onto something, I thought. *Entrepreneurs are total lunatics.*

* * *

By 1978, over 90 percent of American households had a TV.[205] Experts were worried about the dangerous lure into ignorance television offered: "The paralyzing comfort of the armchair in front of the telly." When Joey Tribbiani in the 1990s sitcom *Friends* learned his date didn't have a television at home, he was bewildered. "But what does your furniture point at?"[206]

Like Joey's date, Harper grew up in this world of ubiquitous television with none of his own. He was born in Greeley, an archetypal Colorado town known for having its very own odor hotline residents could call if they smelled something funny.[207]

His mother was a teacher and his father had a small business. "We were not wealthy," Harper described. "We had no money."

"What was growing up in that environment like?" I asked him.

"Well, it made me focus." He shrugged. "I prioritized fun."

His parents didn't care about grades, so Harper chose not to either. For him, grades were like your number of followers on social media: mere vanity metrics. With no television screen to spend his time ogling, Harper explored the world around him. He taught himself to code on a clunky, cubical Apple II. He played LEGO with his brothers. In the process, he let his unfinished homework assignments stack up on his desk.

In college, Harper studied computer science and philosophy. "Those seem like pretty disparate fields," I commented.

"Well, if you look at ancient philosophers and the kind of work they did, a lot of it was in discrete mathematics and logic, subjects that are actually very similar to programming computers." He paused. "But also, I just studied what I wanted to study." It's easier to have fun when you don't overcomplicate the small things.

After college, Harper hopped around. He started his first company, which sold ringtones and wallpapers. He took up professional juggling as part of a group called The Jugglers Against Homophobia. He got a job as a web programmer, and a year later, was fired.

These significant life events are listed on Harper's personal website. In 1978, he was born. In 1984, his house caught on fire, but luckily, his LEGO survived. And in 1990, a year before he hit his teens, he stopped taking himself seriously forever.[208]

It explains his galactic-bananas first impression, but for the rest of us, not taking yourself seriously can feel like a tall order. From achievements shared on social media to trage-dies blasted on the news, we are constantly bombarded by reminders of just how serious life is.

Should it feel like such a tall order?

When something unexpected happens, we shake our heads, wryly remarking that "life is a rollercoaster." But rollercoasters don't exist to justify stomach-wrenching drops. They exist for people to have fun. When an operator straps us into a rollercoaster, they don't yell "watch out for the sudden twists!" They yell "Enjoy the ride!" as our cart rattles down the tracks into the unknown.

Underdogs are particularly bad at following operator advice. When black content creator and activist Luvvie Ajayi landed a book deal for her debut book, she felt she needed the book to blow up. "I put the pressure on myself," she said. "Our failures are considered the rule and our success is considered the exception."[209] Ajayi wanted to be the exception.

In this haste to do well, it is all too easy to disregard fun; can fun and high performance be correlated?

* * *

What do Planters, Wikipedia, and the 2000s fashion industry have in common? They have all dabbled in crowdsourcing.

In 1916, Planters Nut and Chocolate Company ran a contest to find its logo. Fourteen-year-old Antonio Gentile won with his drawing of a friendly peanut who we know today as Mr. Peanut.[210] In 2001, two curious minds came together to create an open-source encyclopedia anyone on the internet could contribute to.[211] In the mid-2000s, this trend of crowdsourcing took the fashion industry by storm.

As the internet entered more and more homes, companies were able to reach the general public quicker than ever before. "Remember outsourcing?" one magazine quipped. "Sending jobs to India and China is so 2003."[212] The new source of cheap labor was everyday people anywhere in the world. With crowdsourcing, companies could make open calls to the public for any kind of task they wanted to be done.

In the fashion industry, this meant the line between designer and consumer was blurring. The old way was to predict what customers wanted. The new way was to ask them.

In New York, you could design your own sneakers by means of touchscreen kiosks glued onto Bloomingdale's store windows. In online fashion communities, you could suggest ideas for exclusive collections from legendary designer Rebecca Minkoff.[213] After decades of brands brainstorming in isolation from their customers, brands could now involve their audience in every step of the process.

The star of this trend? A small company called Threadless. Each week, Threadless creators would submit designs to the platform. The designs with the most votes from the audience were printed onto T-shirts and sold on the website. For every one thousand designs, about one was selected. Their best-selling shirt of all time was called "The Communist Party" and featured some of history's most controversial figures donning party hats and drinking from red Solo cups.

In 2005, Harper joined Threadless as an engineer. "The company was totally bonkers," he described, "in the best way possible." Two years later, he became Threadless's chief technology officer. It's the kind of promotion any professional would swoon at.

"How did you make such a rapid transition?" I asked him.

"I was just in the right place at the right time," he responded. For Harper, the right place was where the fun happened to be.

As other crowdsourcing companies were thinking about how to make their design tools easier to use or how to carry more products, Harper built technology that fostered Threadless's community. Users were encouraged to blog on Threadless forums, create social media content based on their designs, and engage with designers and fellow customers.

As a result of Harper's efforts, Threadless was at the forefront of the crowdsourcing movement by 2009. Technologists and fashion enthusiasts alike fawned over the company. That same year, Harper left.

What happened?

* * *

You can find the same kind of chemical activity in the brains of people who love rollercoasters and shoplifting. They both tend to have higher levels of dopamine.

Rollercoaster riders have suffered strokes, brain deformation, and even death. Yet, at amusement parks, people wait in lines for rollercoasters for up to eight hours. It seems completely irrational—so why do we do it?

We can find some answers in the blood of the riders. Rollercoaster riders often have heightened levels of endorphins, the hormones associated with intense pleasure, but they also have heightened levels of cortisol, the hormone associated with stress.

It turns out not all stress is created equal. Riders experience *eu*stress. *Eu* comes from the Greek word for good, so eustress literally translates to good stress. The high of intense pleasure combined with good stress is enough to keep people waiting in line for hours.[214] The high of innovation is enough to keep entrepreneurs dreaming for years.

In other words, entrepreneurs have more in common with adrenaline junkies than meets the eye: they are both lunatics.

All rollercoasters end eventually. The cart screeches against the tracks before coming to a halt. The dopamine in your brain comes crashing down as you stumble out and face real life again. Then, you brush yourself off and get in line for a different ride. Life isn't a rollercoaster, it's a whole amusement park.

We tend to settle comfortably into stagnation, staying in the same opportunities even if they no longer challenge us to grow. There is no fun staying on a ride once it's ended. When you respect the ride duration, amusement parks open a whole new world of opportunities. Embrace that fluidity.

Harper left Threadless because he knew his ride was over. "The goals I had set for myself were all accomplished," he explained. It made sense for him to leave and seek out a new rollercoaster. In real life, finding that next adventure isn't as easy as walking a few feet over to stand in line.

"I was literally laying on the ground from 2009 to 2011," Harper said. "I call it my vision quest. I was trying to figure out what I was doing and why I was doing it."

He was still on his vision quest two years later when Michael Slaby came knocking. Slaby was the past chief technology officer of Obama for America. He wanted to hire his replacement for Barack Obama's reelection campaign. Harper figured he could help and connect the campaign with some engineers he knew.

It was 2011. Technology was still novel and politics as archaic as ever. Technology was never an internal priority, so past presidential campaigns had all brought it in through external consultants. While Obama's 2008 presidential campaign was praised by many as digitally savvy, most of the team's strides were in social media. In the grand scheme of things, their strides were insignificant. "Facebook was about one-tenth of the size that it is now. Twitter was a nothing burger for the campaign," Teddy Goff, the campaign's digital director, admitted. "It wasn't a core or even peripheral part of our strategy."[215]

This time around, they wanted to be radical.

Harper quickly realized Slaby didn't want to connect with his extensive network in technology. He wanted Harper.

It was a thought that had never crossed Harper's mind. After all, he didn't look the part of a political technologist—he lacked the short-sleeved polos and golf clubs close at hand. The man who had spent his life trying to maximize his fun was hesitant.

His partner and father were both incredulous when they heard his doubts: "'What are you doing? Of course you're doing this." With the same unease of your lone friend screaming before the rollercoaster even begins, Harper got on the ride.

His first day was far from comforting. "Welcome to the team," campaign chief Jim Messina greeted Harper. "Don't mess it up."[216] The stakes of Harper's new job were no longer an unhappy venture capitalist. They were the fate of the entire country.

Creating technologically innovative political campaigns has always been tough. No software engineers want to take a pay cut and move to a new city for a one-year gig.

But Harper's sense of fun was magnetic. "He [Harper] may be like you, but he also juggles better than you, and is wilder than you, more fun than you, cooler than you," *The Atlantic* later described. "He's what a king of the nerds really looks like."[217] And so the nerds filed in. Harper recruited engineers for the campaign from all the top technology companies at the time, from Twitter to Google to Facebook to Quora.

Some days, you would find the team presenting a slide deck with their boss photoshopped as a giraffe. "For some reason, he just doesn't make a great giraffe," Harper laughed. Other days, you would find the team huddled around a PC with furrowed eyebrows trying to build some new software.

What were they building? No precedent existed for a tech-driven political campaign. They certainly couldn't look to the opposing campaign team, who was building a "digitized strike list" that allowed volunteers to update their database as people cast their ballots. Obama's campaign had already built a similar technology in 2008.

This time around, Obama's team wanted to be bolder. If they failed, future campaign managers would assume that tech was better left out of politics. Few people were betting on Harper's success. "Harper is an easy guy to underestimate because he looks funny," one man working alongside the campaign reflected.[218] The pressure was immense.

"How did you figure out what to do?" I asked Harper.

"We didn't really get that no one had done what we were doing," he said, shrugging. "Plus, we were having a lot of fun."

* * *

Let's say you're on a road trip with a friend and you get a flat tire. You have never dealt with one in your life (sorry, mechanics!)

and don't know if it can be fixed. You get out of the car and crouch down to check it out. "It doesn't look too good," you say.

"Well, we have to figure it out or we'll be stranded here forever," your friend responds. "No pressure." She grins. It's a bad pun, but it's enough to break the ice. You both laugh and then get to work on figuring out how to fix the tire.

Most people in this situation never fix the tire because they decide it's impossible at the start. It's easier to do the impossible when you're willing to try, and it's easier to try when you're having fun.

Harper and his team didn't know how impossible their ideas really were, so they built.

They built, as one news outlet calls it, the "most sophisticated email fundraising program ever." They built an analytics software that used data to optimize ad placements, saving the campaign more than $30 billion. They built a tool that alerted supporters on social media when their friends hadn't voted yet. They built one-click purchases for political donations.

By the time election week was upon them, the campaign had integrated technology into every aspect of the strategy. They engaged more volunteers and had more donors than the 2008 cycle. And they enjoyed the entire ride. On November 6, 2012, Obama was reelected for his second term.

Fun is crucial to innovation. Still, not every fun person is changing the world. Clearly, not all fun is created equal. How do you enjoy the ride and innovate while doing it?

GET GOOD

"Is something funny?" teachers often ask sternly when they see someone smiling in class. When we have to describe ourselves to our peers, we are encouraged to use words like "diligent" and "responsible" instead of "funny" and "easygoing." It's been drilled into us since we were children: fun and games don't get you far in life.

It makes sense. Many kids who enjoy playing video games, for example, have lower GPAs on average than kids who don't.[219] That doesn't mean all play is counterproductive to high output, however. Elon Musk, a man who simultaneously serves as the CEO of two multi-billion-dollar companies, tweets frequently throughout the day. His tweets are lighthearted and often nonsensical. Musk doesn't pay attention to the whirlwind he puts his PR team through—he merely enjoys the ride.[220]

So, what's the secret? "You have to get really good at your work," Harper said. "Then, fun cannot get in the way." When you're good at what you do, fun makes a small dent in your productivity. When you're bad, fun makes a hole.

When I was growing up, small animals cluttered my desktop. When I got bored with studying math, I played with them. I gave them personalities and opinions and entire life stories.

I vividly remember one time in seventh grade when I was assigned a particularly dull math project. The toys started as a source of distraction, but eventually, I imagined they were talking about my math project. They made jokes about my teacher as they brainstormed how to help me. It made me laugh and got me the shiny "A" I had been hoping for. Over time, I found that make-believe helped me learn math quicker. When you're already good at something, having fun is less costly, but to *get* good at something, having fun is crucial.

What do you do if you have to do something that just isn't fun?

BRING CAKE

When I used to get sick as a kid, I would insist on having cake. While I hated having the sniffles, desserts never failed to make my eyes light up. At eight years old, I had already learned a fundamental truth of life: everything is fun with cake.

The thing about fun is it's not inherent to certain activities. I have sat around glumly while my friends played laser tag but giggled to myself while cleaning my room. Fun is about the way you approach an activity. Fun is an active effort. Fun is hard work.

There were days in Harper's time as CTO when he would force his team to think about the ways their work could go wrong. Then, he would simulate that exact situation and make them piece together a solution. One of the engineers on the team said it reminded him of his time in the Navy.[221] It was not fun to prepare for the worst.

Harper brought cake.

Cake was a way for the team to celebrate the small wins. When the team sent their application to production, they ate a cake that said "production" on it in sloppy cursive. On the teeth-grinding Election Day, they ate a cake with an adorable pug on it, reminding them to "calm the pug down."

When I first spoke with Harper, I remember thinking to myself, *not everyone is privileged enough to have a fun job.* To some extent, I was right. Most people cannot show up to online meetings muttering about bananas and not face any consequences. Being an accomplished entrepreneur enabled Harper to do things at his whim.

While you can't always do fun things, you can always make an effort to add fun. You can bring cake to stressful meetings or dance at your desk while doing the accounting for your company. If you prioritize fun in your mind, you will find ways to bring it to your work. Grab a slice.

* * *

Adam Smith would have laughed if he saw the duct tape wallets I sold when I was younger. I used to spend over five hours carefully cutting out each individual piece of tape and then sell my precious wallet for twenty-five dollars. In a state where the minimum wage was about ten dollars an hour, I was making less than half of that. The father of capitalism would never understand why I did it.

The inefficiency of my duct tape wallet business never bothered me. My heart leaped in excitement when a stranger approached me to buy a wallet. I was in a state of bliss every time I planned a new wallet. They were customized to the person who bought them, so each wallet told a unique story. My own wallet has a hot cup of coffee carefully carved onto it. The steam from the coffee takes the figure of a lion. I smile every time I take it out and someone notices. "It's supposed to represent the fact that coffee turns me into a lion," I say.

Duct tape wallets taught me everything I know about business. When your job is to sell a craft many people made as a kid, you have to get good at marketing. When your process is inherently inefficient, you have to learn operations. As the people around me watched my business intuition grow stronger, they felt I was wasting my talents. "Have you ever looked into drop shipping?" one uncle asked me at a family dinner. "It's a big thing now and makes money much quicker."

I never paid much attention to such suggestions, because duct tape wallets had something drop shipping never would: they were fun. Many of my best ideas came when I was hunched over my desk, with a craft knife in hand, slowly cutting through a piece of duct tape. Joy keeps our minds pliable. It helps us innovate.

As underdogs, our chances at innovative success are low by nature of the word "underdog." Enjoying the ride, then, is more important for us. If the process isn't fun and the desired outcome isn't likely, it's not worth it.

Harper launched a new company called Modest in 2015. A few months later, it was acquired by PayPal.

Harper officially started the company in 2012 right after Obama's reelection. But between founding the company and being acquired, his website doesn't mention much about what happened. Instead, it talks about an app he built that automatically deletes friends randomly from your Facebook account. It talks about his first visit to Australia. It talks about wrapping his parents' car in zebra stripes. It's this flexibility and sense of fun that allowed Harper to innovate so quickly, going from a stealth start-up to being acquired by one of the biggest financial technology companies in the world.

As you embark on this crazy journey of innovation, follow the pull of fun. Bring joy and experience it. Be the lunatic Michael Seibel knows you are. Do things worth hunching over your desk at three a.m. for a few measly dollars or none. Do things that would make Adam Smith scoff. As any good rollercoaster operator would tell you, "Hold on tight and enjoy the ride."

ENJOY THE RIDE

- You don't need an elaborate reason for every decision you make. Sometimes, "it's fun" is enough.

- Embrace fluidity. Think of your life as a series of roller-coasters in an amusement park. When one ride ends, you hop off and get on another.

- If you've been in one place for a long time, reflect on if it's still challenging you to grow. If it's not, it might be time to pursue something new.

- It's easier to try the impossible when you're having fun.

- Work on getting good at what you love. When you're good at something, fun helps you innovate instead of hampering your productivity.

- Fun takes active effort. If you're stuck doing something that's not fun to you, add the elements of fun yourself.

CONCLUSION

SOME PARTING WORDS

———

Lean into the system that disadvantages you. It's the radical idea Facebook COO Sheryl Sandberg proposed when she wrote the book *Lean In* in 2013. As one of the most powerful women of her time, Sandberg used the book to outline principles for other women to achieve corporate success. If their workplace does not support feminine qualities, they should be more masculine. If there is no seat for them at the table, they should pull one over.[222]

As underdogs, we have all been told to "lean in." Since we became old enough to feel the weight of obstacles, we were told to jump over them. It makes sense—if you conform to the status quo, you are better able to succeed within it. And I have nothing but respect for Sandberg's ability to navigate a corporate landscape so hostile to women.

Innovation is a wholly different game. Your job isn't to succeed in the status quo, it's to create new norms.

At Facebook, when the product team was about to launch a new feature, they all moved into one room so they could talk in close proximity; as the team grew rapidly, one room could no longer fit everyone. It seemed impossible, a tradition from their start-up days that was not plausible for a corporation. Still, the team was determined. So, over the weekend, they built a loft that housed desks on two levels.[223]

When we enter a room, we see the walls around us as a constraint, but walls also come with ceilings that open a whole world of possibilities. The team innovated by thinking outside the constraints of two dimensions. They thought outside the odds.

Throughout this book, we have also learned to think outside the odds. We learned that underdogs are given many constraints and these constraints can boost our innovation. They help us think differently and stand out, but only if we're intentional about it.

Life gives us a starting point with the context of our environment, and we learned to play those cards. We explored places bigger than where we are now. This is where the frontier lies. We sought out the parts of these environments that foster innovation, its pearls. Not everything around us was useful for our innovation, so we learned to be our own air purifiers.

To innovate, we have to wander. We thought about our conversations and how to ask questions that helped us explore what was around us. Once we discovered new spaces through curiosity, we threw dinner parties and started our own conversations there. We learned that what we say "yes" and "no" to guides our success in this process. Conversations are two-sided, so we listened for the sake of listening. Conversations are three-dimensional, so we learned to be seen in order to be heard.

We were now equipped with the tools to move through our lives at large. We knocked on doors, pursuing opportunities that offered no clear reward. We learned that sometimes after doing so much, success can still seem hopeless. That's when we have to defy life's pincers, relentlessly taking small steps toward our goals. Packed with so much information, we found that a little bit of naivety helps us stay focused and be bold. However this whole adventure goes, the most important part is that we enjoy the ride.

It can feel overwhelming to look back on all of it now. Luckily, this book isn't going anywhere. As I told you at the beginning of all this, *Think Outside the Odds* is your toolkit. You don't need to cram every chapter into your memory right now. Instead, reflect on everything you read. Which stories resonated the most deeply with you? Which problems felt most relevant to where you are right now? Which bullet points made you want to take notes?

Whatever lessons come to mind, write them down on a sticky note and place it above your desk to glance at every day. That is all you need right now.

Different chapters of your life will present you different problems requiring different tools to solve. When that happens, I hope you come back to this book. You will find one or two chapters that feel especially relevant to your life at that time. Grab those tools then. Take a second to refresh your little sticky note.

As with any pesky home improvement project, remember that sometimes you'll need more than just the tools in your toolbox to get the job done.

Many of the entrepreneurs I spoke with were hesitant about being featured in this book. *I don't know if I was really an underdog,* they told me. *I still had privileges.* They told me stories of mockery and self-doubt and impossibilities, but they also told me stories of expensive educations and the life-changing belief of one person in their abilities.

This is all to say that there is an element of luck in becoming a successful entrepreneur. Many hardworking, passionate people never achieve it. You can foster innovation, but you cannot induce it. You can think outside the odds, but you cannot make the odds cease to exist.

In choosing to live intentionally, you have to accept that many things are out of your control. Sometimes, innovation depends on such things. Sometimes, it depends on luck. This book cannot change that.

So why try at all?

When you choose to live intentionally, you maximize your chances of getting lucky. You prime your life for innovation. Take the leap because you're worth that better shot at your dreams, but be kind to yourself. You are embarking on a crazy adventure of making the impossible, possible. It's okay to feel frustrated, to fumble, to fail. Breathe.

You've now heard stories of people starting global movements with shoelaces and revolutionizing the housing industry after growing up homeless. You've gone on this winding journey of oysters and fancy dinner parties and spiraling rollercoasters. You've got a toolkit for intentionality in your back pocket. It's time to use it. Go out and make some magic. Make these tools rust with use. I am rooting for you.

Your journey to achieve the impossible has just begun.

ACKNOWLEDGMENTS

There are many people who contributed to making this impossible dream of mine possible. From strangers on the internet telling me they were excited for me to friends and family letting me borrow their time to ask questions and get feedback, thank you. I am humbled by and grateful for the outpouring of support and love. What follows only scratches the surface of the people who touched this book.

Thank you to my family, who were quick to wipe off the *are you crazy?* look from their faces when I first told them I wanted to write a book.

To my mom, who has been a constant source of inspiration. I watched her start her own school and become an entrepreneur as I explored the world of entrepreneurship myself through writing. In between her classes and chores, she never hesitated to offer me some matcha or a hug.

My dad, who listened enthusiastically to whatever the latest developments in my book were, regardless of how many hours past midnight it was. When I was impatient to find quick solutions to obstacles, he was patient with offering ideas. When I was uncertain, he was certain.

Arav Dayal, my brother, who sat by my side and helped me brainstorm everything from chapter titles to citations to detailed all-nighter plans. He is almost seven years younger than me but gave me advice with the wisdom of someone at least seven years older.

My extended family, who picked up my spontaneous phone calls for help and sent me constant encouragement. They have told me I could be an author since I was in middle school, and while their faith may have been misplaced, their belief in me kept me going.

My grandparents, who asked me eagerly each time I called, "When will your book come out?" Thank you for your enthusiasm and love.

My late *nana*, or maternal grandpa, who inspired my chapter on curiosity and shared my love for words.

To Roshan Rao for believing *Think Outside the Odds* was powerful, months before it was anything at all. For driving me to coffee shops and picking me up from them, for editing countless emails and drafts, and for always knowing what I needed to write at my best.

My family friends, who are family in everything but blood. For being some of the earliest supporters of this book and rooting for me from the very beginning.

My friends, who encouraged me, brought me coffee, and stuck with me when I was not as responsive as I could have been.

Grace Gooneratne, Smera Patil, Samhi Saiba, Syna Sharma, Harsh Thakkar, Reshma Varma, Pakhi Singh, and Dan Zhu for reading over my drafts. The words of support and jokes you left on the documents I shared always made late-night editing sessions a little easier. Dheeraj Varma, who was tireless with helping me brainstorm cover and layout ideas.

The people I interviewed whose vivid storytelling made this book all the easier to write: Ali Abdaal, Doug Augustine, Aisha Bowe, Tammy Camp, Alfonso Cobo, Lisa Seacat DeLuca, Jesse Draper, Kinsey Grant, Daniel Gross, Daniel Kasidi, Phillip Kim, Akshay Kothari, Alexandria Lafci, Angela Luna, Umaimah Mendhro, Harper Reed, Shetal Shah, Alice Waters, and Alex Wieckowski. Thank you for giving me your precious time, being patient with my constant follow-up emails, and believing in the mission of this book.

Thank you to all of my teachers, professors, and mentors. Mike Grandinetti, who gave me encouragement and opportunities to grow. Ms. Hedges, who helped me find my writing voice. Umaimah Mendhro, who showed me the power of kindness and generosity. The faculty at UC Berkeley, who always inspire me to learn in and outside of the classroom. The teachers at John P. Stevens High School, who first showed me how to chase after my dreams.

To Eric Koester, Brian Bies, and the entire team at New Degree Press, without whom this would not have been possible. My editors, Al Bagdonas, Kathy Wood, Ryan Porter, Carol Shetler, and Joshua Rivedal, for being honest with me and helping me relentlessly refine my message. The artists, designers, marketers, and proofreaders who touched the book with their work.

The strangers who became friends during this time, from people on Twitter to subscribers of my newsletter: thank you for reaching out and for supporting someone you only knew through a screen.

The incredible researchers whose work I leaned on heavily to make my arguments: thank you for making the internet a joyful place and for giving me many rabbit holes to go down.

The coffee shops who gave me lattes to keep me awake and conversations to keep me inspired: thank you for giving me a place to write for hours on end. To name a few: The Edison Automat, Frappe Joe's, CLO, Lokal, Cafenated, Romeo's Coffee, 1951 Coffee Company, and Caffè Strada.

And lastly, thank you to everyone who joined the community around this book, preordered copies, and took a chance on my work. Thank you for engaging with my ideas and giving me endless support:

Shraddha Agrawal	Alvaro Morales
Vadini Agrawal	Arpana Naithani
Vinaya Akavoor	Shruti Narain
Shalini Aneja	Rithika Neti
Sathish Arya	RD Nigam
Doug Augustine	Ami Parikh
Joyce Beverly	Rebecca Pu
Swati Bhatnagar	Bala Rajaraman
Vineesh Bhatnagar	Arhant Rao
Simran Buddhadev	Deepak Rao
Tia Chen-Wong	Jayati Rao
Sara Cheung	Roshan Rao
Alfonso Cobo	Lukas Rosenstock
Aparna Das	Madhura Saha
Shobha Dasari	Abhinav Sahay
Bireshwar Dayal	Samhitha Saiba
Mohini Dayal	Nagesh Sarma

Sanjeev Dayal

Veneeta Dayal

Andy Dent

Monique Derflinger

Charlie Fu

Rahul Garg

Maya Haylock

Jennifer Hedges

Alex Hillman

Dan Himelstein

Poonam Jain

Richa Jethwa

Vidisha Jha

Sheetal Kamani

Vijay Kamarajugadda

Surabhi Karambelkar

Daniel Kasidi

Sadaf Khan

Eric Koester

Abhas Kumar

Brajesh Kumar

Shashwat Kumar

Srishti Kumar

Surbhit Kumar

Sanjay Lall

Varsha Lall

Hyewon Lee

Matthew Lee

Karen Lin

Grace Lu

Praveen Saxena

Ria Sharma

Sandhya Sharma

Mayurkumar Shetye

Harpreet Singh

Pakhi Singh

Sukhbir Singh

Akanksha Sinha

Kirti Sinha

Rajnish Sinha, FL

Rajnish Sinha, NJ

Shweta Sinha

Mariana Somma

Briahna Sparks

Summer Stewart

Marissa Strang

Mahesh Swaminathan

Priya Tejwani

Geetika Thakur

Sandhya Todi

Dheeraj Varma

Jayanti Varma

Kiran Varma

Nikhil Varma

Snehanand Varma

Swati Varma

Reshma Varma

Shruti Venkat

Bharat Gopal Verma

Diwakar Virnave

Angela Luong   Helen Wang
Ifeoma Madu   Madeleine Wong
Ragini Mallick   Cort Worthington
Miguel Marcos   Jeffrey Zhang
Sanjeev Mehta   Daniel Zhu
Leah Modica

Thank you all for helping me think outside the odds.

ENDNOTES

——

1   Marcus Aurelius and Charles Reginald Haines, Meditations (Cambridge, Massachusetts: Harvard University Press, United States of America, 1916).

2   "They Say Einstein Said," UCLA Computer Science Department, accessed March 2, 2021.

3   Oprah Winfrey, "Oprah Winfrey's Commencement Address," May 30, 1997.

4   Monica Villavicencio, "A History of Dogfighting," NPR, July 19, 2007.

5   "Underdog," in The Shorter Oxford Dictionary, 1983.

6   "The underdog effect: Definition, limitations, and motivations" (master's thesis, University of South Florida, 2005).

7   Ashley Turner, "Why there are almost no Starbucks in Australia," CNBC, July 25, 2018.

8   Joey Watson, "Australian Coffee Is the New Gold Standard — and Not Just for 'Chin-Stroking Inner-Urban Instagrammers,'" ABC News, December 28, 2019.

9   "Our History," Australian Specialty Coffee.

10   Turner, "Why there are almost no Starbucks in Australia."

11   Michael Zakkour, "Why Starbucks Succeeded in China: A Lesson for All Retailers," Forbes, August 24, 2017.

12   "Starbucks in China," Starbucks, accessed June 25, 2021.

13   Martin Kihn, "'Outside the Box:' The Inside Story," Fast Company, June 1, 2005.

14   Daniel Schacter, "Are All of Your Memories Real?" TED-Ed, 2020.

15   Dennie van Dolder, "Hard Evidence: Is Poker a Game of Chance or Skill?" The Conversation, March 26, 2015.

16   If playing online poker was your full-time job, this would be equivalent to more than a month on the job.

17   Dolder, "Hard Evidence: Is Poker a Game of Chance or Skill?"

18   David Apostolico, *Lessons from the Pro Poker Tour: A Seat at the Table with Poker's Greatest Players* (Lyle Stuart, 2006), 6-7.

19   *The Mersey Sound*, (BBC Television, 1963).

20   Colin Bertram, "How the Beatles Got Together and Became the Best-Selling Band of All Time," *Biography*, August 13, 2019.

21   "The Simplicity and Sophistication of the Beatles, with Aaron Krerowicz," Musical U, January 11, 2020.

22   William D. Moylan, "How the Beatles Took Recording Technology to a New Level in 'Abbey Road,'" *Smithsonian Magazine*, October 2, 2019.

23   Peter Barrett et al., "Summary Report of the HEAD Project Clever Classrooms," 2015.

24   Daniel Lubetzky, "Daniel Lubetzky, Founder and Executive Chairman of KIND Snacks," interview by Goldman Sachs, *YouTube,* December 18, 2019.

25   Daniel Lubetzky, "How KIND Built a Billion-Dollar Business with Heart," interview by Inc. Magazine, September 13, 2018.

26   Lubetzky, "Daniel Lubetzky, Founder and Executive Chairman of KIND Snacks."

27   Myelle Lansat and Richard Feloni, "A CEO Who Based His $700 Million Company in Pittsburgh Says He's Getting Employees Who Want to Work in Tech but Avoid the Bay Area," *Business Insider,* June 30, 2018.

28   The churn rate here means the rate at which employees left the company. If words that sound like math make you shudder, essentially, Von Ahn's employees were sticking around.

29   Alice Hancock, "Duolingo's Luis von Ahn: Luring Tech Talent to Pittsburgh," *The Financial Times*, August 26, 2018.

30   When Draper says there's no shortage of talent, what she means is the average venture capitalist sees 200-500 companies a year. She sees about five thousand.

31   "Johnny Moss The 'Grand Old Man' Of Poker," *Vicepost*, (May 21, 2009), retrieved November 6, 2010.

32   Elon Musk, "Elon Musk - CEO of Tesla Motors and SpaceX," interview by Sal Khan, YouTube, April 22, 2013.

33   Michael Sheetz, "SpaceX Launches Two NASA Astronauts to Space for the First Time in Historic US Mission," CNBC, May 30, 2020.

34   Musk, "Elon Musk - CEO of Tesla Motors and SpaceX."

35   Musk made his initial calculations for the cost of raw materials on the most basic rocket shop possible, which sold for $25 million. NASA's typical order tends to be more complex than this, hence the $90 million figure.

36   Michael Sheetz, "NASA's Deal to Fly Astronauts with Boeing Is Turning out to Be Much More Expensive than SpaceX," CNBC, November 19, 2019.

37   That said, I do think their fresh perspective could be better used on something other than space tourism. If you're curious to understand why, I highly recommend looking into the social and environmental costs of recreational space travel.

38   I'll be referring to Y Combinator by its abbreviation, YC, throughout the book.

39   An accelerator is a cohort-based program for entrepreneurs to grow their ideas within a fixed amount of time.

40   Jeremy Brown, "100 Startup Accelerators around the World You Need to Know About," Crunchbase, August 8, 2019.

41   Fun fact: Steve Jobs was known for cruising around the Valley in his Mercedes with no license plate. He almost ran Daniel over during these forty-eight hours. Daniel will meet Jobs in a less life-threatening form later in his story.

42   A lot of the iPhone's machine learning abilities were created under Daniel's leadership: from the way it can guess the contact name of a new number you're texting to the way Siri bickers effortlessly with you.

43   Gina Kolata, "Obesity Spreads to Friends, Study Concludes," *New York Times*, July 25, 2007.

44   Nicholas A. Christakis and James H. Fowler, "The Collective Dynamics of Smoking in a Large Social Network," *New England Journal of Medicine* 358, no. 21 (May 22, 2008); J. H Fowler and N. A Christakis, "Dynamic

Spread of Happiness in a Large Social Network: Longitudinal Analysis over 20 Years in the Framingham Heart Study," BMJ 337, no. 2 (December 4, 2008): a2338–38.

45   Kolata, "Obesity Spreads to Friends, Study Concludes."

46   Aimee Groth, "You're the Average of the Five People You Spend the Most Time with," *Business Insider,* July 24, 2012.

47   David Einstein, "Kamran Elahian's Startup Momenta Was a Huge Flop – but Now He Has 3 Ventures on the Fast Track," SFGATE, October 1, 1998.

48   Erin Schulte, "Self-Proclaimed 'Fail Factory' 500 Startups' Recipe for Success," *Fast Company*, November 14, 2011.

49   Bill Murphy Jr., "Google Says It Still Uses the '20-Percent Rule,' and You Should Totally Copy It," *Inc Magazine,* November 1, 2020.

50   "Pioneer - the Network for Ambitious Outsiders," Pioneer, accessed January 11, 2021.

51   This is the same Paul Graham who chased Daniel down after rejecting his pitch for YC.

52   Paul Graham, "Cities and Ambition," Paul Graham's Personal Website, May 2008.

53   If you want to get fancy, you can also call the "d.school" the Hasso Plattner Institute of Design.

54   This idea came a few years before Facebook actually created its own in-app timeline feature.

55   If you're curious about why this might happen, take a look at your spam folder. If it's anything like mine, it'll have a lot of emails about romance and dating. You might also see an abundance of links and exclamation points. An overenthusiastic parent's message can seem similar to unsolicited emails from dating websites to your average spam filter.

56   Daniel J. Levitin, *The Organized Mind: Thinking Straight in the Age of Information Overload* (Dutton, 2015).

57   Eric Ries, *The Lean Startup: How Today's Entrepreneurs Use Continuous Innovation to Create Radically Successful Businesses* (Crown Business, 2011).

58   Jayadevan PK, "Earning His Stripes," Purdue Alumnus, March 30, 2018.

59   Aliya Uteuova, "The World Is Your Oyster," *The Catch* 6, no. 10 (2018): 2.

60   In the fishing world, prying open an oyster is called "shucking." Amateur shuckers often get away with no gloves, but the professionals wear heavy-duty shucking gloves. They reduce your risk of injury and even give you a better grip.

61   Leo Tolstoy, *The Power of Darkness* (A Word To The Wise, 2013).

62   Nicole Spector, "How to Train Your Brain to Accept Change, According to Neuroscience," NBC News, November 12, 2018.

63   In other words, if you've been reading this book slouched over your desk, this is your sign to try reading it on the floor or standing up.

64   Michael Clarke, "The Digital Revolution," ScienceDirect, 2012.

65   Claire Lisa Evans, *Broad Band: The Untold Story of the Women Who Made the Internet* (New York, New York: Portfolio/Penguin, 2018), 26.

66   "Adele Goldberg," University of Maryland, College Park Computer Science Department, accessed December 30, 2020.

67   "When Women Stopped Coding," NPR, October 17, 2014.

68   A shout out is due to Lisa, who woke up early just for our call.

69   "Apple Computer Ad 1985 JH," YouTube, 1985.

70   NPR, "When Women Stopped Coding."

71   Noam Cohen, "Michael Bloomberg, the Original Tech Bro," *Wired*, February 14, 2020.

72   David Lynch, "Interview With David Lynch: His Mission to Change the World Through Meditation," interview by Marianne Schnall, HuffPost, December 9, 2014.

73   See Chapter 3.

74   Gabriel Andrade, "Girard, Rene," Internet Encyclopedia of Philosophy, accessed December 27, 2020.

75   Erin L. Kelly et al., "Changing Work and Work-Family Conflict," *American Sociological Review* 79, no. 3 (May 4, 2014): 485–516.

76   Eugene Kim, "This Quote Perfectly Sums up How Yahoo Killed Flickr," *Business Insider*, August 12, 2014.

77   E. Pronin, D. Y. Lin, and L. Ross, "The Bias Blind Spot: Perceptions of Bias in Self Versus Others," *Personality and Social Psychology Bulletin* 28 (2002): 369 - 381.

78   It takes a certain amount of privilege to be able to leave your environment. If you can't leave, reflect back on Chapter 1, where Umaimah Mendhro faced a similar struggle stuck in Pakistan for many years. She air purified by distancing herself physically from her environment when she could and exploring ideas in the safety of her own home. Many years later when she got the resources to leave (filter), she did.

79   Ron Miller and Alex Wilhelm, "Salesforce Buys Slack in a $27.7B Megadeal," *TechCrunch*, December 1, 2020.

80   Susan Engel, "But Why? Children's Curiosity in the Classroom" (University of Pennsylvania School of Arts & Sciences), accessed June 30, 2021.

81   Prachi E. Shah et al., "Early Childhood Curiosity and Kindergarten Reading and Math Academic Achievement," *Pediatric Research* 84, no. 3 (April 26, 2018): 380–86.

82   Ibid.

83   Benjamin Mullin, "Business Insider Parent Nears Deal to Buy Controlling Stake in Morning Brew," *Wall Street Journal*, October 14, 2020, sec. Business.

84   Hayley C. Cuccinello, "Millennial Newsletter Morning Brew Hits 1 Million Subscribers," Forbes, February 7, 2019.

85   Robert A. Butler, "The Effect of Deprivation of Visual Incentives on Visual Exploration Motivation in Monkeys.," *Journal of Comparative and Physiological Psychology* 50, no. 2 (1957): 177–79.

86   Tracey Lien, "Peter Thiel's Resume Includes PayPal, Facebook and Supporting Trump. And He's Coming to L.A.," *Los Angeles Times,* February 15, 2018.

87   Michael P. Gibson (@William_Blake), "One day I walked into the office and Peter Thiel was in a conference room with 7 scholars. I asked his assistant what they were doing," Twitter, December 21, 2019.

88   Kinsey Grant, "Mark Cuban on COVID Responses: Perfection Is the Enemy of Progress," March 26, 2020, in *Business Casual*, podcast, 21:00.

89   Kinsey Grant, "Arianna Huffington: Maybe We Shouldn't Follow the Leader?" May 12, 2020, in *Business Casual*, podcast, 09:01.

90   Kinsey began exploring Josh's email list when online communities were experiencing a surge due to the COVID-19 pandemic. Companies were struggling to figure out how to engage their customers digitally but Josh had cracked the code years ago.

91   Stephanie Vozza, "Are You Genetically Predisposed for Your Career?" *Fast Company*, February 27, 2018.

92   Steve Jobs, "Commencement Address," *Stanford News* (Stanford University, 2005).

93   Walter Isaacson, "How Steve Jobs' Love of Simplicity Fueled a Design Revolution," *Smithsonian* (Smithsonian Institution, September 1, 2012).

94   "The Science of Curiosity," Britannica's Curiosity Compass, accessed June 30, 2021.

95   Dopamine is the neurotransmitter associated with pleasure and reward in our body. Learning what a "skeuomorph" is rewarding for our brains.

96   Tommy C. Blanchard, Benjamin Y. Hayden, and Ethan S. Bromberg-Martin, "Orbitofrontal Cortex Uses Distinct Codes for Different Choice Attributes in Decisions Motivated by Curiosity," *Neuron* 85, no. 3 (February 2015): 602–14.

97   Weingarten, Elizabeth. "Who Asks Questions, and What It Tells Us." *Behavioral Scientist*, June 19, 2019.

98   Blaise Pascal, *Pascal's Pensées* (Project Gutenberg, 1958).

99   Jordan A. Litman, "Relationships between Measures of I- and D-Type Curiosity, Ambiguity Tolerance, and Need for Closure: An Initial Test of the Wanting-Liking Model of Information-Seeking," *Personality and Individual Differences* 48, no. 4 (March 2010): 397–402.

100 If you want to go down the same rabbit hole, look up "The History of the Ice Cream Truck" on the *Smithsonian Magazine* website.

101 "Over 3,770 Migrants Have Died Trying to Cross the Mediterranean to Europe in 2015," United Nations International Organization for Migration, December 31, 2015.

102   Grace Lee Boggs and Scott Kurashige, *The next American Revolution: Sustainable Activism for the Twenty-First Century* (Berkeley: University of California Press, 2011), 159.

103   *MSN Encarta,* "Louis XIV," retrieved January 20, 2008.

104   Peter Mcneil and Giorgio Riello, *Luxury: A Rich History* (Oxford, United Kingdom: Oxford University Press, 2016).

105   If you're a programmer, you might find this definition of short-circuiting simplistic. I've distilled it to what is most relevant in this context.

106   Salk Institute, "Associative Memory — Learning At All Levels," ScienceDaily, accessed June 1, 2021.

107   Brody Ford, "IAC's Vimeo Raises New Funds at $6 Billion Valuation," Bloomberg, January 25, 2021.

108   Nilay Patel, "How Anjali Sud Reinvented Vimeo," *The Verge*, April 20, 2021.

109   "Vimeo, Inc. 2021 Investor Day Presentation," U.S. Securities and Exchange Commission, March 24, 2021.

110   Douglas MacMillian, "Facebook's Missing Millionaires," Bloomberg, March 8, 2012.

111   "Stereotype Threat," National Institute of Health, June 30, 2017.

112   "Stereotype Threat Widens Achievement Gap," American Psychology Association, July 15, 2006.

113   Jesse Pujji, "Is Zuckerberg a Visionary?," LinkedIn, June 25, 2021.

114   "Inc. 5000 2020: Introducing the 5,000 Fastest-Growing Private Companies in America," *Inc Magazine,* 2020.

115   Tony Robbins, "You Have the Right to Say No," The Official Website of Toby Robbins, August 17, 2015.

116   Ruth Umoh, "Billionaire Richard Branson Reveals Why He's Such a Huge Fan of Always Saying 'Yes,'" CNBC, December 18, 2017.

117   "SMART Goals: A How to Guide," University of California Office of the President, 2016.

118   Mark Murphy, "'SMART' Goals Can Sometimes Be Dumb," Forbes, January 8, 2015.

119   Charles Darwin, *The Expression of the Emotions in Man and Animals* (New York: D. Appleton and Company, 1913), 272.

120   Charukesi Ramadurai, "Cracking India's Mystifying 'Nod Code,'" BBC News, July 23, 2018.

121   Margaret E. Backman and Bruce W. Tuckman. *Journal of Educational Measurement* 9, no. 2 (1972): 161-62, accessed June 30, 2021.

122   Richard Freeman, "Creativity And Diversity: How Exposure To Different People Affects Our Thinking," Hidden Brain, interview by Shankar Vedantam, NPR, July 27, 2020.

123   "New Research Shows That Close Intercultural Relationships Can Enhance Individual Creativity and Innovation Potential," Columbia Business School, June 28, 2017.

124   I met Angela (Chapter 6) through Alfonso. They are both Parsons alumni who explore design in distinct ways.

125   Here, a subreddit refers to a community on the online forum, Reddit.

126   Virginia Heffernan, "Our Best Hope for Civil Discourse on the Internet Is On... Reddit," *Wired*, Winter 1AD.

127   r/changemyview," Reddit, accessed January 5, 2021.

128   "Inspirational and Leadership Quotations," University of California, San Diego School of Medicine, accessed January 5, 2021.

129   "The Three A's of Active Listening," Queens University of Charlotte, January 4, 2021.

130   G. J. Stephens, L. J. Silbert, and U. Hasson, "Speaker-Listener Neural Coupling Underlies Successful Communication," *Proceedings of the National Academy of Sciences* 107, no. 32 (July 26, 2010): 14425–30.

131   Tom D. Lewis and Gerald Graham, "7 Tips for Effective Listening: Productive Listening Does Not Occur Naturally. It Requires Hard Work and Practice," *Internal Auditor* 60, no. 4 (August 2003).

132   "The Three A's of Active Listening."

133   Confirmation bias is our tendency to interpret new information in a way that conforms to our current beliefs and values.

134   The fact that you're reading this book right now is a testament to Augustine's kindness. I met him because he was one of the earliest backers of *Think Outside the Odds*.

135   David Perell, "How to Cure Writer's Block," David Perell's Personal Website, accessed January 9, 2021.

136   James Clear, "'Atomic Habits' Author James Clear: 'I'm Never Far From a Good Idea,'" interview by Polina Marinova Pompliano, YouTube, January 12, 2021.

137   Daniel P. McVeigh, "An Early History of the Telephone: 1664-1866: Robert Hooke's Acoustic Experiments and Silent Inventions," Columbia University, retrieved January 15, 2013.

138   Nicole Krauss, *The History of Love* (New York: W. W. Norton & Company, 2015).

139   McVeigh, "An Early History of the Telephone."

140   Piotr Winkielman and Yekaterina Gogolushko, "Influence of Suboptimally and Optimally Presented Affective Pictures and Words on Consumption-Related Behavior," Frontiers in Psychology 8 (January 29, 2018).

141   Yingying Ma, "Can More Pictures Bring More Readership?: An Examination of the 'Picture Superiority Effect' in the News Consumption Process," Procedia - Social and Behavioral Sciences 236 (December 2016): 34–38. We saw this in action earlier with Angela Luna, when a picture of a child drove her to dedicate her career to the refugee crisis.

142   "Providing Care for Immigrant, Migrant, and Border Children," *Pediatrics* 131, no. 6 (May 6, 2013): e2028–34.

143   Brandy R. Maynard et al., "Bullying Victimization among School-Aged Immigrant Youth in the United States," *J Adolescent Health* 58, no. 3 (March 2016): 337–44.

144   Susan M. Swearer and Shelley Hymel, "Understanding the Psychology of Bullying: Moving toward a Social-Ecological Diathesis–Stress Model.," American Psychologist 70, no. 4 (2015): 344–53.

145   This is a huge feat. For reference, I spent four years learning a martial art under a trained instructor and still didn't receive my black belt.

146   Matthew Buzzi, "Apple MacBook pro vs. Microsoft Surface Laptop 3: Which 13-Inch Premium Laptop Is Tops?," PC Magazine, May 12, 2020.

147   "Gartner Says Worldwide PC Shipments Grew 32% in First Quarter of 2021," Gartner, April 12, 2021.

148   "Apple's Technological Lag Is Starting to Show," IndustryWeek, July 27, 2016.

149   Steven Greenhouse, "2010 Economy Changed Many Americans' Lives," interview by Neal Conan, Talk of the Nation, November 30, 2010.

150   Taylor Lorenz, "Everyone's Playing Among Us," New York Times, October 19, 2020, sec. Style.

151   Jo Craven McGinty, "Is Your Attention Span Shorter than a Goldfish's?," Wall Street Journal, February 17, 2017, sec. Page One.

152   "Twitter for Business," Twitter, accessed December 26, 2020.

153   Lorenz, "Everyone's Playing Among Us."

154   Lydia Dishman, "The Science of Why We Talk Too Much (and How to Shut Up)," *Fast Company,* June 11, 2015.

155   D. I. Tamir and J. P. Mitchell, "Disclosing Information about the Self Is Intrinsically Rewarding," *Proceedings of the National Academy of Sciences* 109, no. 21 (May 7, 2012): 8038–43.

156   Eric Blattberg, "The Demographics of YouTube, in 5 Charts," Digiday, April 24, 2015.

157   "How Much Do Youtubers Make & How to Become a Youtuber," MintLife Blog (Intuit, January 9, 2020).

158   Li Jin, "The Passion Economy and the Future of Work," Andreessen Horowitz, October 8, 2019.

159   "Awesome Products Designed by Independent Artists," Redbubble, accessed May 25, 2021.

160   "About," Patreon, accessed May 25, 2021.

161   Daniel Sanchez, "Less than 2% of Content Creators on Patreon Earn Monthly Minimum Wage," Digital Music News, January 2, 2018.

162   "Knock Down Ginger," Project Gutenberg, World Heritage Encyclopedia, accessed December 31, 2021.

163   Pujji, "Is Zuckerberg a Visionary?"

164   *Show Your Work* by Austin Kleon is a great read if you're trying to figure out the whole "being a creative" thing out.

165   Holly Firmin, "StudyTube and the Fetishisation of Productivity," *Ebb Magazine,* April 16, 2020.

166   Tyler Perry, "F.O.C.U.S. | Follow ONE Course until Successful," YouTube, September 4, 2013.

167   Tim Ferriss, "Fear-Setting: The Most Valuable Exercise I Do Every Month," The Blog of Author Tim Ferriss, May 17, 2017.

168   Ibid.

169   "Study: Brain Battles Itself over Short-Term Rewards, Long-Term Goals," Princeton University PR, October 14, 2004.

170   If you're feeling overwhelmed by all the opportunities you could be pursuing, pause and revisit the ideas in Chapter 7 (Nod with Purpose). You can't say yes to everything—and that's okay. Part of balancing doors with windows is being selective about the doors you choose to knock on. Think of doors as low-effort opportunities to help you discover your "What If" goals and supplement the time you spend on your SMART steps.

171   Laura Joffe Numeroff, *If You Give a Mouse a Cookie* (New York: Laura Geringer Book, An Imprint Of Harpercollins Publishers, 1985).

172   Peter Dizikes, "When the Butterfly Effect Took Flight," MIT Technology Review, February 22, 2011.

173   Phil Edwards, "Claw Machines Are Rigged — Here's Why It's So Hard to Grab That Stuffed Animal," Vox, June 3, 2015.

174   Tim Ferriss, "Why Bigger Goals = Less Competition," The Blog of Author Tim Ferriss, June 19, 2008.

175   "Gender Insights Report," LinkedIn Talent Solutions, 2019.

176   Tyler Green et al., "Perceptions of Short-Term Medical Volunteer Work: A Qualitative Study in Guatemala," *Globalization and Health* 5, no. 1 (February 26, 2009): 4.

177   Sharon McLennan, "Medical Voluntourism in Honduras: 'Helping' the Poor?," SAGE Journals 14, no. 2 (March 26, 2014): 163–79.

178   Fun fact: One of Alexandria's close friends from college was U.S. Representative Alexandria Ocasio-Cortez.

179 Thomas Mussweiler and Kai Eptude, "Relatively fast! Efficiency advantages of comparative thinking," American Psychological Association, 2009.

180 Julie Scelfo, "Suicide on Campus and the Pressure of Perfection," *New York Times,* July 27, 2015.

181 Kia Kokalitcheva, "Red Cross Spent Half a Billion Dollars to Build Six Homes in Haiti," *Time,* June 3, 2015.

182 It's been a while since we've talked about YC. In case it slipped your mind, YC stands for start-up accelerator Y Combinator.

183 Heather Taylor, "Cost of Constructing a Home," National Association of Home Builders, November 2, 2015.

184 Adele Peters, "Take a Look at the Vision for the World's First 3D-Printed Neighborhood," *Fast Company,* May 9, 2019.

185 "New Story: Most Innovative Company," *Fast Company,* accessed June 30, 2021.

186 Rebecca Aydin, "How 3 Guys Turned Renting Air Mattresses in Their Apartment into a $31 Billion Company, Airbnb," *Business Insider,* September 20, 2019.

187 Drake Baer, "Inside the Video Game Roots of Slack, Everyone's Favorite Workplace Messaging App," *Business Insider,* March 17, 2016.

188 Casey Newton, "Creamery Is Deal Central for SF Techies," SFGATE, July 14, 2012.

189 Brian Chesky, "Airbnb's Brian Chesky in Handcrafted," interview by Reid Hoffman, May 3, 2017.

190 Peter Whoriskey, "Why Your 'Organic' Milk May Not Be Organic," *Washington Post,* May 1, 2017, sec. Business.

191 Shane Hamilton, "The Economies and Conveniences of Modern-Day Living: Frozen Foods and Mass Marketing, 1945–1965," The Business *History Review* 77, no. 1 (2003): 33–60.

192 Seth Rosenfeld, "Mario Savio's FBI Odyssey / How the Man Who Challenged 'the Machine' Got Caught in the Gears and Wheels of J. Edgar Hoover's Bureau," SFGATE, October 10, 2004.

193 Austin Kleon, Show Your Work! : *10 Ways to Share Your Creativity and Get Discovered* (New York, NY: Workman Publishing Company, 2014).

194   David Kamp, "Cooking up a Storm," *Vanity Fair,* October 10, 2006.

195   Carl Schramm, "Why Creating a Business Plan Is a 'Waste of Time,'" Knowledge @ Wharton, May 24, 2018.

196   Anthony K. Tjan, "Great Businesses Don't Start with a Plan," *Harvard Business Review,* May 16, 2012.

197   Kamp, "Cooking up a Storm."

198   Libby Simon, "How Information Overload Affects the Brain," Psych Central, March 15, 2018.

199   "E-Mails 'Hurt IQ More than Pot,'" CNN, April 22, 2005.

200   Wendy Suzuki, "Fear Shrinks Your Brain and Makes You Less Creative," interview by Carolyn Milton, April 18, 2018.

201   "Maria Montessori | Biography & Facts," in Encyclopedia Britannica, 2019.

202   "The Edible Schoolyard Project" Edible Schoolyard, 2021.

203   Carolyn Lochhead, "President Honors Alice Waters' Vision of Ethical Food with Medal," SFGATE, September 11, 2015.

204   "Michael Seibel | 2020 40 under 40 in Tech," *Fortune,* 2020.

205   "Number of TV Households in America 1950-1978," *The American Century,* Washington and Lee University, accessed June 3, 2021.

206   Andrew Anthony, "A History of Television, the Technology That Seduced the World – and Me," *The Guardian,* September 7, 2013.

207   A. J., "It Has an Odor Hotline, and 10 Other Fun Facts about Greeley," *New Country 99.1,* April 19, 2021.

208   Harper Reed, "Harper Reed's Personal Website," 2021.

209   Rhonesha Byng, "Failure Is Not an Option: The Pressure Black Women Feel to Succeed," Forbes, August 31, 2017.

210   Kathleen Franz, "Mr. Peanut and Antonio Gentile: A Trademark That Defined a Life," National Museum of American History, May 6, 2014.

211   "Wikipedia," in Encyclopedia Britannica, August 1, 2018.

212   Jeff Howe, "The Rise of Crowdsourcing," *Wired,* June 1, 2006.

213 Cate T. Corcoran, "Reinventing Fashion via Crowdsourcing," *Women's Wear Daily*, July 26, 2010.

214 Richard Stephens, "The Psychology of Roller Coasters," *The Conversation*, July 11, 2018.

215 Alexis C. Madrigal, "When the Nerds Go Marching In," *The Atlantic*, November 16, 2012.

216 Admittedly, this is the family-friendly version of what Messina actually said.

217 Madrigal, "When the Nerds Go Marching In."

218 Ibid.

219 Jancee Wright, "The Effects of Video Game Play on Academic Performance," *Modern Psychological Studies 17*, no. 1 (2011).

220 Taylor Lorenz, "Elon Musk: Memelord or Meme Lifter?," *New York Times*, May 7, 2021, sec. Style.

221 Madrigal, "When the Nerds Go Marching In."

222 Sheryl Sandberg, *Lean In: Women, Work, and the Will to Lead* (New York: Alfred A. Knopf, 2013).

223 Andrew Bosworth, "The Hacker Way," Andrew Bosworth's Personal Website, September 8, 2014.